LOVE 'EM

'EM

AND

LEAD

'EM

WRITTEN AND ILLUSTRATED BY
**PAUL B. MALONE III**

# LOVE 'EM

A "HOW TO" BOOK
ON LEADERSHIP
FOR EVERYONE

AND

# LEAD 'EM

**SYNERGY PRESS**
ANNANDALE,
VIRGINIA

LOVE 'EM AND LEAD 'EM

By Paul B. Malone III

Published by: Synergy Press
3420 Holly Road
Annandale, VA 22003

Book Design by Kevin Osborn, Arlington, Virginia.
Typesetting by Monotype Composition Co., Inc., Baltimore, Maryland.
Printing by McNaughton & Gunn, Inc., Ann Arbor, Michigan.

Library of Congress Cataloging in Publication Data.
Malone, Paul B. III
  Love 'Em and Lead 'Em
1. Leadership
2. Management
3. Human Behavior
4. Organizational Behavior
Library of Congress Catalog Card Number 86-60237

ISBN 0-9616548-0-5 Softcover
ISBN 0-9616548-1-3 Hardcover

**TO ANN**

**WHO HAS PATIENTLY PROVIDED LOVE AND SUPPORT AS**

**I TRIED TO PRACTICE WHAT I PREACH.**

# ACKNOWLEDGMENTS

My debts associated with this work go back many years. I owe a great deal to the United States Army, the finest organization I know, which introduced me to the concept of leadership and provided me the opportunity to put what I knew and what I sensed in my heart into practice. My personal experiences, successful and otherwise, plus my observations of military leaders, good, bad and indifferent, are very much a part of this book. Later, in career number two, George Washington University and its administration, faculty and students provided the environment where the research, testing and writing of this work became a possibility.

I am particularly indebted to fellow academicians at George Washington University whose guidance, both supportive and cautionary, was essential to this, my first major literary effort. These included Dean Norma Loeser, Associate Dean Ben Burdetsky and Assistant Dean Marvin Katzman plus Professors David Brown, Roy Eastin, Jerry Harvey, Gordon Lippitt, John Lobuts, Harry Page and Michelle Slagle, all of the School of Government and Business Administration, and Professor Herman Hobbs of Columbian College. Special thanks go to Professor Susan Tolchin whose encouragement at a critical time helped keep the production moving.

My project was most generously supported by members of the staff of the School of Government and Business Administration whose efforts contributed materially to the book. The list includes some very talented and supportive people—John Casey, Stephanie Husik, Fred Ross, Diane Bongiorni, Bill Skilton and, very critically toward the end, Diana and John Del Vecchio.

Since this book is designed to inform aspiring leaders, I needed inputs from young students who were totally involved in the learning and development process. These were provided by a group of outstanding teaching assistants whose research and opinions were vital—Laura Bos, Patti Jackomis, Dave Tobey, Steve Yalof, Lori Marcus and Sandra Harlen.

I took advantage of the generosity of many friends, some very old and dear, as I developed this work. My special thanks go to Otis Moran, Wesley Jones, Joseph Dooley, Bill Brown, Kevin and Marguerite Kirk, Peter and Christine Kunz, Larry and Barbara Putnam and Lauren Thayer. Jack and Carol Burkheimer "blessed" my use of humor. Finally, Dan Rapoport, President of Farragut Publishing Company, provided essential guidance just when I needed it.

My family endured quite a bit as I engaged in this "labor of love". My best friend and only wife, Ann, was my inspiration, guide and finest critic. Our older son, Paul IV, a captain in the Army, tested my ideas with "the troops". Our daughter, Marylee, and her husband, Jim, and our younger son, Pat, were constant sources of creative ideas and very valuable support. Finally, my mother, Ethel Malone, provided a helpful hand at a critical time. Actually, *Love 'Em and Lead 'Em* is very much a *Malone Family* effort.

# CONTENTS

# MEET BERT AND BERTHA

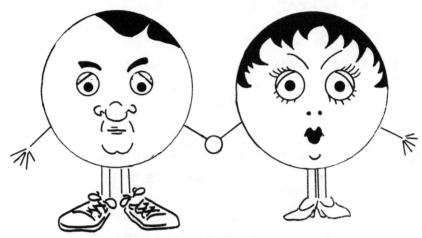

THEY LOOK LIKE BALLS

LiTTLE BALLS

THAT IS BECAUSE THEY HAVE NO POWER

THEY WANT POWER
POWER TO LEAD OTHER PEOPLE

THEY WOULD LIKE TO BECOME BIG BALLS

*Malons*

THAT'S WHY THEY BOUGHT THIS BOOK
LET'S FOLLOW BERT AND BERTHA AS THEY GROW
MAYBE YOU CAN GROW TOO.

# INTRODUCTION

Why on earth would someone want to read a book on leadership? Think about it for a moment. Unless you plan to live a life of solitude in a cave, you will spend the rest of your life either leading or being led or both. With this in mind:

- Do you want to change something in this world that needs changing?
- Do you want to achieve something you can't do alone?
- Do you enjoy working with people and perhaps even helping them with their lives in the process?
- Are you looking for a place in society where you can possibly gain respect, admiration, personal fulfillment and, perhaps, a bunch of ready cash?
- Are you looking for a little excitement, uncertainty, frustration and challenge?
- Do you sense a need for power?
- Are you a potential leader who would like a general understanding of what leadership is all about?
- Are you a follower who would like to know what people are doing to you so you can take charge, turn the tables and drag your organization out of the ashes?
- Are you lonely?

**HAVE I GOT A BOOK FOR YOU!**
Any one of the motives mentioned above could stimulate YOUR interest in this book. Now, it's up to ME to make sure that your investment in time and money is cost effective.

**COMMENT:**
Allow me at this time to introduce Bert and Bertha. They appear holding hands together on the opposite page. They will be joining you in this study of leadership. If you're alert, you'll note that they're drawn in the shape of balls. I'll be using balls frequently throughout the book in

reference to people. Balls are easy to draw. More than that, balls are, in many ways, like people. It's tough to stack balls (get them organized); they tend to roll all over the place in different directions. Further, you can inflate, dribble, kick, stroke and manipulate balls—just like people. For illustrative purposes, the little balls will be subordinates and the big balls will be the leaders. Enough on balls for now; we'll see more of them later on.

The book has three parts, each with a specific purpose:
• PART A provides you a basic practical and, to a very limited extent, theoretical understanding of leadership and closely related subjects. I promise to take it easy on the theory. Whether you've had plenty of experience at leading or are brand new to the subject, PART A provides an essential foundation for what follows.
• PART B provides you MY philosophy of leadership and, thus, a basis for comparison with others. I don't claim that my philosophy will work for you, but many successful people are now considering similar approaches to leading people.
• Part C provides you a technique for developing YOUR personal philosophy of leadership and, thus, your basic approach to dealing with people, particularly subordinates.

This book contains three basic themes:
• First, leading people nowadays is considerably more challenging and demanding than it has been in the past.
• Second, participative leadership (sharing power and decision making authority with subordinates) is no longer an option available to a leader— it is a MUST in advanced societies. The question is not WHETHER to allow for participation but HOW MUCH participation to allow.
• Third, leaders must know themselves in order to be successful in influencing others. Leaders must take the time to develop their own personal philosophies of leadership AND THEN go to the trouble to share selected portions of their philosophies with their subordinates.

My personal philosophy is embodied in "my commandments" that follow in this introduction and are discussed in Part B of the book. They're written to amuse you slightly, but they also express my personal beliefs. I've been moderately successful using them. I'll try to persuade you that they have merit. However, I don't expect you to adopt my philosophy—GO OUT AND DEVELOP YOUR OWN! Part C of the book is designed to help you do this, but it will require some intense soul-searching and analysis on your part. If you're not up to searching your soul right now, don't stop—there's lots here that should stimulate your thinking without even touching your soul.

There are many books on the subject of leadership. This one is intended to be different. It reflects my personal bias that most people are "good" given the proper environment. Part of that environment is often provided by the leader. When "good" people receive "good" leadership, everyone gets a "warm" feeling—THAT'S GOOD ALL OVER!

Another bias you might detect is my conviction that life, work and learning should be FUN. I had fun writing this; I hope you enjoy reading it. Part of this book is written in a "tongue-in-cheek" manner based on the philosophy that LEARNING WITH LEVITY *is* a productive mix. I have intentionally introduced some silly sayings and people with weird names to make some points while reducing the tedium associated with "serious stuff". Recognizing that much learning today is transmitted through the visual senses, I have drawn some cartoons (nothing hilarious, but they might make you smile) to reinforce some major learning points. I recognize that this approach may turn you off since no two people agree precisely about what's really "funny". I agree wholeheartedly with Gordon Lippitt who wrote, "Humor punctures our pretenses. People have the capacity to laugh at themselves, take themselves less seriously and become less threatening to others."[1]

I realize that many disagree with such a frivolous approach and insist that LEARNING MUST INVOLVE PAIN. If, deep down, you feel that smiles and laughter constitute "unnatural acts", please get your money back and invest instead in a well-written tragedy.

I recognize that my approach to this subject involves risks. My attempts to entertain you while you read this should NOT lead you to believe that leading people is frivolous or insignificant. Leading is serious business. The world desperately needs people with integrity who can influence the behavior of others. The world is becoming more and more interdependent; very few actions of any significance are achieved by people functioning alone. However, we are faced with what might be called a crisis of leadership, particularly at the national level. This crisis is described by Michael Maccoby as follows:

> The American public is dissatisfied with its leaders and confused about the kind of leaders we need. . . . But there are no ideal national leaders. There is no model of leadership that inspires America during a time of changing social character; we are distrustful of authority and still believe in the idea of self-fulfillment.[2]

John Naisbitt, author of *Megatrends*, views "the problem" from a different perspective:

> In the United States, there has been a fundamental mismatch between traditional American love of personal liberty and the top-

down, authoritarian manner in which the American workplace has operated. Employees habitually surrender the most basic rights, to include free speech and due process, for example,when at work each day.[3]

Laurence Peter and Raymond Hall, in their book, *The Peter Principle*, view leadership in large, bureaucratic organizations as virtally a "lost art" as they note that

Most hierarchies nowadays are so encumbered with rules and traditions, and so bound by public laws, that even high employees do not have to lead anyone anywhere, in the sense of pointing out the direction and setting the pace. They simply follow precedents, obey regulations, and move at the head of a crowd. Such employees lead only in the sense that the carved wooden figurehead leads the ship.[4]

If the observations, above, are accurate, one might question whether leadership is really necessary. John W. Gardner lamented that "we are immunizing a high proportion of our most gifted young people against any tendencies to leadership. . . . They [the scientists and professionals] envisage a world that does not need leaders, only experts."[5] Perhaps some of our educators agree. Most courses in management allocate very little attention to the subject of leadership. I shudder to think of the consequences if the enemies of this nation sensed that the United States were a leaderless mass.

Most leaders have power. Power is often abused. Those with the ability to lead can generate both good and evil. We are all aware of cases where some basically good people did some awful things in response to the influence of an evil but effective leader. With this in mind, I hope that people with the values of Adolph Hitler or affiliations with the Mafia do not read this book.

Americans are swallowing a bit of "humble pie" and are examining how others, to include the Japanese, work with people. People of many nations still flock to America to learn how to *manage*. There's far less interest in how we *lead*.

This is a "how to" book on leading. It should HELP you to examine yourself and to work on an approach to leadership that suits your own unique personality, skills and experience. The world is aching for people who can put such understanding to practical use.

## COMMENT:

Wow! I told you I planned to mix levity and learning, and the past few pages have been "heavy stuff". Sorry, but those quotes deal with some real and profound problems. Note that the "authorities" don't always agree. We'll be dealing with these issues and others throughout the book.

I don't claim to have the "school solution" because there is none, but I have some thoughts based on considerable research and practical experience that should be of help to you.

Enough of the introductory ritual: let's get on to the meat or message of the book—"my commandments" that are discussed in Part B of the book. Remember, they are just one man's approach to leading. It's interesting how they came to me:

**IT WAS THE BEST OF NIGHTS AND THE WORST OF NIGHTS. THE MOON WAS FULL. THUNDER ROARED, AND LIGHTNING FLASHED IN THE DISTANCE. MY MIND THROBBED WITH THE THRICE-DIS-TILLED QUINTESSENCE OF EMOTIONAL ECSTASY, AND A VISION MATERIALIZED. FROM ATOP A MOUNTAIN A MAN WITH WHITE ROBES DESCENDED. HE APPEARED TO BE A COMBINATION OF LEE IACOCCA AND CHARLTON HESTON WITH A FLOWING GRAY BEARD. HE WAS CARRYING TWO LARGE STONE TABLETS PLUS A BIG BOOK. NO, AS MY VISION CLEARED, I COULD SEE THAT THE TABLETS WERE NOT TABLETS AT ALL—THEY WERE MASSIVE COMPUTER PRINT OUTS. AND THE MOUNTAIN WAS MADE, NOT OF ROCK, BUT OF A HUGE PILE OF PEOPLE WHO HAD BEEN GUIDED IMPROPERLY BY LEADERS OF THE PAST. THE VENERA-BLE MAN REFERRED TO HIS NOTES, ADJUSTED HIS SPECTACLES AND HIS SHORTS, CLEARED HIS VOICE AND BEGAN TO SPEAK. BEHOLD, HE PROVIDED THE STRUGGLING MASSES OF THE WORLD WITH . . .**

## MALONE'S COMMANDMENTS OF LEADERSHIP

1.  Thou shalt develop a personal philosophy of leadership, share part of it with thy subordinates and live by it, recognizing that thou canst fool none of the people none of the time.

2.  Thou shalt view thy subordinates as the children of God and behave accordingly in the exercise of thy power, recognizing that power corrupts and thou art corruptible.

3.  Thou shalt not bring sadness and gloom unto the workplace. Instead, thou shalt endeavor to enrich the life of each subordinate thou toucheth.

4.  Thy mind shalt dwell in the future whenever possible. Thou shalt not make a decision a subordinate could make just as well.

5.  Thou shalt not direct thy subordinates without explaining WHY.

6.  Thou shalt tolerate and even encourage some degree of conflict, disagreement and error and combat the afflictions of doppelgangeritis, numberungus and pole vaulting over mouse droppings.

7.  Thy hand shalt include both a palm and knuckles. Thou shalt reward frequently and in public BUT thou shalt also possess the innards to punish in private with blinding speed and surgical skill.

8.  While thou shalt maintain some "psychological distance" from thy subordinates, thou shalt make thyself available to those in trouble, offering thy hand, thy ear, thy heart and thy handkerchief but never thy money. In the process, thou shalt resist the temptation to play God or psychiatrist unless thou art properly anointed or qualified.

9.  Thou art responsible for everything thy organization does or fails to do. When things are "gangbusters", thou shalt step back and introduce thy subordinates. When everything turns brown, thou shalt step forward and take thy licks.

**AS THE VISION BEGAN TO FADE, I WAS REMINDED NOT TO COMPETE WITH MOSES WHO HAD TEN COMMANDMENTS AND THAT TOO MUCH "THOU" AND "THY" IS TEDIOUS AND BORING AND WILL TURN OFF MY READERS.**

## NOTES

[1]Gordon L. Lippitt, "Putting Life in Perspective", a collection of essays in 1982-1983 editions of the *Training and Development Journal*, p. 12.

[2]Michael Maccoby, *The Leader* (New York: Simon and Schuster, 1981), p. 13.

[3]John Naisbitt, *Megatrends* (New York: Warner Books, Inc., 1982), p. 181.

[4]Laurence J. Peter and Raymond Hall, *The Peter Principle* (New York: Morrow, 1969), pp. 70, 71.

[5]John W. Gardner, "The Antileadership Vaccine", in William A. Nielander and Max D. Richards, (Eds.) *Readings in Management* (3d Ed.) (Cincinnati,OH: South-Western Publishing Company, 1969), pp. 27, 29.

# PART A

# BACK TO BERT AND BERTHA

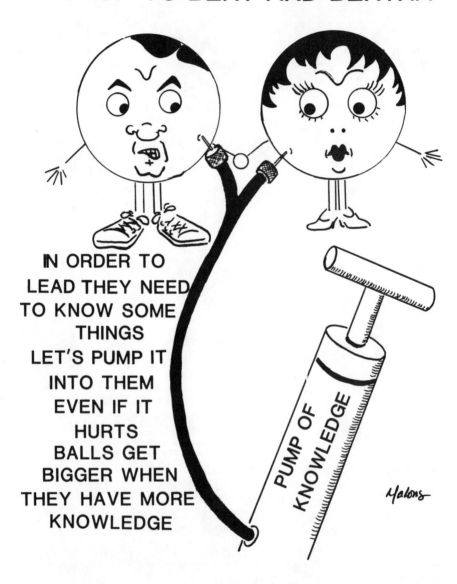

IN ORDER TO
LEAD THEY NEED
TO KNOW SOME
THINGS
LET'S PUMP IT
INTO THEM
EVEN IF IT
HURTS
BALLS GET
BIGGER WHEN
THEY HAVE MORE
KNOWLEDGE

PART A

# DEFINITIONS, THEORIES, CONCEPTS AND TRENDS

## OBJECTIVES OF PART A

Every house needs a foundation. This part of the book provides an essential foundation for what follows. It includes definitions, theories, concepts and trends that are essential to the understanding of what leadership is all about.

A complete treatment of the subject of leadership would fill a library. My approach will be selective and general and, thus, incomplete. You'll have to trust me that I've selected the proper high points.

## ORGANIZATION OF PART A

Chapters in this part of the book are organized as follows:

• Chapter One defines the term, leadership, and discusses key definitions and concepts associated with leadership.

• Chapter Two provides a historical view of the changing environment within which leaders operate and identifies issues confronting today's leaders.

• Chapter Three examines the subject of human motivation as it applies to the role of the leader.

• Chapter Four reviews some of the theories and basic approaches to the study of leadership effectiveness.

**COMMENT:**

Our hero and heroine, Bert and Bertha, on the opposite page, are basically lovable but not particularly effective. They need some fundamental knowledge if they are to acquire power, to be able to influence other people, TO BECOME BIG BALLS. We are now going to give them a four-chapter blast of this. We will be pumping it into them very fast. Some minor pain may be involved, but pain will be followed by pleasure when they put this to productive use because BIG BALLS GET THINGS DONE! Join Bert and Bertha and watch yourself grow too!

# CHAPTER ONE

# WHAT'S LEADERSHIP ALL ABOUT?

"I happen to *know* a little about leadership. . . . You do not *lead* by hitting people over the head. Any damn fool can do that, but it's usually called 'assault' and not 'leadership'. . . . I'll tell you what leadership is. It's *persuasion* and *conciliation*—and *education*—and *patience*."

General of the Army Dwight D. Eisenhower[1]

## WHAT IS LEADERSHIP?

It would be great if there were one standard definition of the term, leadership. Unfortunately, this isn't the case. Almost everyone who writes on the subject seems to invent his/her own. Apparently, this makes some of them feel good. I guess I'm no exception so here goes with a relatively simple definition that I plan to use from now on: LEADERSHIP = GETTING PEOPLE TO DO THINGS—WILLINGLY. Leadership involves the following:

• A group of two or more people who interact directly in some location (let's call the location an "environment"; that's what the "big boys" do).

• One or more persons (the leader(s)) who influence the behavior of others.

• One or more persons (the subordinate(s)) who respond to the influence of the leader(s).

• Some action by the group.

## WHAT ARE THE DISTINCTIONS BETWEEN LEADERSHIP AND MANAGEMENT?

Some pretty knowledgeable people use the terms interchangeably. I think they're wrong. The process of management involves a variety of activities to include PLANNING, ORGANIZING and CONTROLLING. Some of these activities include direct interactions between managers and their subordinates; some do not. Leadership, a vital sub-set of the management process, relates to the DIRECT INTERPERSONAL INTERACTIONS that influence human behavior. MANAGEMENT focuses on the *logical, rational and cerebral*; LEADERSHIP focuses largely on the *emotional and the interpersonal*. Warren Bennis, an eminent authority on the subject, acknowledged that "probably more has been written and less known about leadership than any other topic in the behavioral sciences."[2]

## COMMENT:

Does this mean that more Americans should be brushing up on their leadership skills? I think many should. Tom Peters and Nancy Austin, in their book, *A Passion for Excellence*, express this more strongly:

> . . . the concept of leadership, is crucial to the revolution now under way—so crucial that we believe the words "managing" and "management" should be discarded. "Management", with its attendant images—cop, referee, devil's advocate, dispassionate analyst, nay sayer, pronouncer—connotes controlling and arranging and demeaning and reducing. "Leadership" connotes unleashing energy, building, freeing and growing.[3]

If management and leadership are unique, a good question might be: "Could a good leader be an ineffective manager and vice versa?" Very possibly. Consider the young lieutenant who inspired his soldiers to charge a hill despite withering fire from the enemy. After their heroic sacrifice and extraordinary performance, they discovered to their chagrin that they had charged the WRONG HILL! On the other hand, an effective manager who is short on leadership abilities might be successful if he/she had few subordinates or if he/she had a deputy who was an effective leader.

## PEOPLE

Frederick Taylor, famous for his theories on scientific management, is also associated with the ECONOMIC MAN approach to human motivation. Taylor's ECONOMIC MAN was quite simple; he worked for tangible rewards, primarily money. The more money you offered, the harder he would work.[4] People have criticized Taylor for his over simplified view of people, but one must recognize that most working people during Taylor's time (the early 1900's) were living at the subsistence level. When one is just barely making a living, his/her behavior is reasonably predictable—a few bucks waved under his nose will definitely get his attention.

Taylor's ECONOMIC MAN model is no longer appropriate for a modern advanced society. Most people have been elevated above bare subsistence levels and have been provided some sense of security. Under such conditions, factors other than tangible rewards motivate behavior. Taylor's ECONOMIC MAN has been replaced by the COMPLEX MAN approach to human motivation. The COMPLEX MAN approach recognizes that *each and every human being is unique, distinct and different.* Just as every person has unique fingerprints, he/she has unique attitudes, values, expectations and goals that have been conditioned primarily by past experiences. Compared to ECONOMIC people fearing possible starvation, COMPLEX people are extremely unpredictable. When such COMPLEX people gather in groups, the potential variations of group behavior are virtually limitless. Harnessing their energies for some common purpose can be challenging.

## PEOPLE IN GROUPS

Among the basic needs common to most people is the need for AFFIL-IATION with other human beings. Based on this need, people will assemble in groups. In the process, they may be willing to give up some of their freedom—which many of them treasure dearly—in order to join or remain with the group. Often, they will allow one or more individuals within the group to dominate group behavior. These "dominators" become the leaders. Most groups of this nature that form BASED ON PEOPLE'S INSTINCTIVE ATTRACTION TO ONE ANOTHER are referred to as INFORMAL GROUPS.

## FORMAL GROUPS

Let us now turn to the other basic type of group, the FORMAL GROUP. Very few people in a complex, interdependent society work alone. People join groups in order to make a living or to achieve some well-identified objective. These people join FORMAL organizations. In a FORMAL organization, the higher organization, rather than the group members, normally designates the group leader(s). Further, the FORMAL organization is likely to demand more of the group member—thus denying more freedom—than the INFORMAL group. The FORMAL GROUP usually offers some form of tangible reward—frequently money—to compensate for the demands on its members and thus make membership "worth it". The FORMAL GROUP member will be continually comparing the costs versus the benefits of group membership. Based on that comparison, the member can:

- Leave the FORMAL GROUP and seek opportunities elsewhere OR
- Remain with the FORMAL GROUP and do the *minimum* in order to maintain membership OR
- Remain with the FORMAL GROUP and commit himself/herself totally to the objectives of the organization.

**COMMENT:**

Referring to the three alternatives, mentioned above, it is appropriate to identify a much-used term associated with the workplace—the "motivated worker". FOR OUR PURPOSES a "motivated worker" is *not* the worker who is motivated to arrive and depart work on time and to do the *minimum* (the second example, above). A "motivated worker" is not only physically involved in his/her work, but is also mentally and emotionally involved in the work. A "motivated worker" is committed to *improving performance*. "Motivated workers" and effective leaders make great teams.

I can sense some wretching among my readers at this point: "Hold on, what have you been smoking? Do you actually expect my workers to be emotionally involved in their work and committed to improving perform-ance? The next thing you'll be saying is that they should look forward to Monday mornings so they can come to work. That's fairy tale nonsense."

Not necessarily. Keep reading; I'll show you how.

## THE LEADERSHIP PROCESS

As mentioned before, the process of leadership requires two basic ingredients—people and an environment. Figures 1-1 and 1-2 illustrate the first step in the leadership process, the formation of the group.

Note that Figure 1-1 depicts a FORMAL GROUP with a designated leader (bigger ball) and a well-defined environment (the triangle). In this case, the FORMAL GROUP is part of a larger formal organization; the leader of the FORMAL GROUP is a subordinate in the larger structure, above, and a vital link between his/her subordinates and those above.

In contrast, Figure 1-2 depicts an INFORMAL GROUP without a leader in this case (all balls the same size) and with an ill-defined group environment. Such a group could be a car pool, people who meet daily in the cafeteria or office mates who would love to see their supervisor transferred to Outer Mongolia.

In the cases of both the FORMAL and INFORMAL group, people *voluntarily* enter the group environment, at least on a trial basis. Note that the arrows emanating from the balls (group members) point in a variety of directions; these are COMPLEX people, each with his/her own attitudes, values, expectations and goals. Since joining a group involves some loss of personal freedom, the question among the balls is, DO THE BENEFITS JUSTIFY THE COSTS?

**COMMENT:**

Take the case of Lolita Lovely (a small ball) who has just gotten a job at Roy Rancid's Restaurant (FORMAL GROUP). Roy (a big ball) demands a lot of his employees. After a few hours, Lolita growls, "Man, this job is the pits! Scrub this, clean up that—all for a lousy minimum wage. I can

# FIGURE 1-1
## FORMATION OF THE FORMAL GROUP

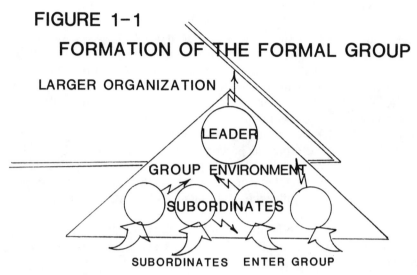

LARGER ORGANIZATION

LEADER

GROUP ENVIRONMENT

SUBORDINATES

SUBORDINATES ENTER GROUP

# FIGURE 1-2
## FORMATION OF THE INFORMAL GROUP

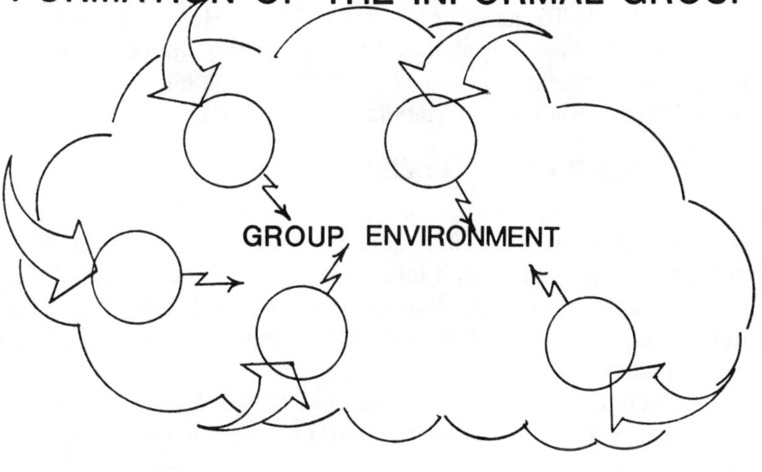

GROUP ENVIRONMENT

get just as much on welfare and still see 'General Hospital' on TV."
Apparently, Lolita doesn't consider the benefits associated with group
membership worth the sacrifices; she's ready to exit the environment and
return to "General Hospital".

Let's now focus on the FORMAL GROUP. With group members'
arrows pointed in a variety of directions as they are in Figure 1-1, very
little common purpose can be achieved. It is the leader's job to influence
the group members to modify their behavior—in essence, to "BEND
THEIR ARROWS"—to contribute to the purposes of the FORMAL
organization. This process involves three basic steps:
  • INTERACTION within the group to identify group objectives.
  • ACTION by the group to proceed toward some objective (ideally
that identified by the leader and the FORMAL organization).
  • REACTION by members of the group to the two previous steps.
This REACTION will influence subsequent INTERACTIONS and AC-
TIONS by the group.
  The process within INFORMAL GROUPS is usually similar except
that some initial INTERACTIONS are necessary to identify the group
leader or leaders.

**COMMENT:**
Thus, we see that leaders are big balls who go around bending arrows
of other people. How effective are you at doing that? How would you like
your arrow bent? To quote from the Big Book, "He who bends arrows for
a living must never forget that he is grabbing people in very tender
places—their attitudes, values, goals and aspirations. By all means, wear
gloves." (Small Paul to the Valedictorians, 23:91.)

# LEADERSHIP EFFECTIVENESS

B.M. Bass identified various classifications of leadership results:
  • "Unsuccessful leadership" occurs when the subordinates refuse to
change their behavior to that identified by the leader (Figure 1-3).
  • "Successful leadership" occurs when the behavior of the group
actually changes to that identified by the leader *as a result of the leader's
efforts* (Figure 1-4).
  • "Effective leadership" is "successful", BUT it also involves something more. Not only does the behavior of the group change in the desired
direction *but members of the group sense personal satisfaction and
reward as a result of their group activities* (Figure 1-5). In the case of
"effective leadership", the INTERACTION, ACTION, REACTION
sequence has contributed to increased willingness by members of the
group to follow the leader.[5]

# LEADERSHIP RESULTS

FIGURE 1-3

### UNSUCCESSFUL LEADERSHIP

FIGURE 1-4

### SUCCESSFUL LEADERSHIP

FIGURE 1-5

### EFFECTIVE LEADERSHIP

SUCCESSFUL PLUS

## COMMENT:

Note that, based on the definitions provided above, the lieutenant who led the charge on the WRONG HILL, mentioned previously, was a "successful" leader—his soldiers followed him despite the risks. However, unless we're dealing with very slow or suicidal soldiers, it is highly unlikely that he would be classified as "effective". "He's a nice chap, but my mother didn't bring me up to charge the wrong hill". The lieutenant's next charge, if any, is likely to be a solo act. This brings up a case worth considering. Can a leader be "effective" if the organization fails to meet its objectives?

Take, for example, the case of Festus Fungus, varsity football coach for the past ten years for Hideawee High somewhere in middle America. Coach Fungus' record has been far from illustrious—every game lost except for one forfeit. The closest game each season for the Hideawee Heifers (they used to be called the Bulls, but the name was changed recently by a unanimous vote of the school board) is that with the junior varsity team which is usually a cliff-hanger. Festus tells his team to play and they do; Festus tells his team to win and they don't. Is Festus an "unsuccessful" leader or not? Based on America's dedication to short-term, quantifiable results, it's unlikely that Festus will be nominated for Coach of the Year. However, there may be other criteria that should be considered. As Dickie Dildu, graduating senior, remarked, "Coach Fungus learned us to lose with dignity—and we got a lot of practice at that". When dealing with a complex subject such as leadership, many things must be considered; nobody can win them all.

## BASIC LEADERSHIP STYLES

Subsequent chapters go into detail concerning various approaches to GETTING PEOPLE TO DO THINGS—WILLINGLY. However, it is appropriate at this time to introduce four BASIC STYLES of leadership.

● If the leader turns to his/her subordinates, identifies the objectives for the group and insists that the group proceed to those objectives, the style would be considered AUTHORITATIVE (Figure 1-6).

● If the leader asks the opinions of group members concerning group objectives and then makes the decision after considering their opinions, this style would be considered CONSULTATIVE (Figure 1-7).

● If the leader actually allows subordinates to participate in the decision making process while retaining full responsibility for the decision, this style would be considered PARTICIPATIVE (Figure 1-8).

● Finally, if the leader intentionally allows subordinates to "do their own thing" (assuming that they don't need the leader's guidance), this style would be classified as LAISSEZ FAIRE (Figure 1-9).

## FIGURE 1-6

## AUTHORITATIVE LEADERSHIP

"THERE'S ONE WAY...MY WAY.
YOU'VE GOT A JOB TO DONE.
NOW GET IT DID!"

FIGURE 1-7

CONSULTATIVE LEADERSHIP

"I'D LIKE YOUR ADVICE
BEFORE I MAKE THE DECISION."

## FIGURE 1-8

## PARTICIPATIVE LEADERSHIP

## "ON SECOND THOUGHT, FELLOWS, LET'S ALL MAKE THE DECISION TOGETHER."

FIGURE 1-9

LAISSEZ FAIRE LEADERSHIP

"NATURALLY, YOU PROFESSORS KNOW YOUR JOBS. I WOULDN'T PRESUME TO TELL YOU HOW. DO WHAT YOU THINK IS BEST AND LET ME KNOW IF YOU NEED HELP."

## POWER TO INFLUENCE THE ACTION OF SUBORDINATES

How do "big balls" get their "little balls" to "bend their arrows"? To put it more politely, how do leaders influence others, their subordinates, to modify their behavior to contribute to the goals of the organization? The answer is POWER—the ability to obtain dominance over others. If subordinates whose motives are based on their own self-interests are to engage in "unnatural acts"—doing something for the good of the organization—they must sense some compelling reason to do so. J.R.P. French and Bertram Raven identified six bases of power available to the leader.[6]

● REWARD POWER—Reward power is derived from the belief *in the mind of the subordinate* that compliance with the wishes of the leader will result in rewards or benefits the subordinate values.

● COERCIVE POWER—Coercive power is derived from the perceived ability of the leader to punish or deny rewards to those who won't comply with the leader's wishes.

● LEGITIMATE POWER—Legitimate power is associated with the status, position or rank of the leader. In many cases, the subordinates will acknowledge that the leader has the "right" to make demands based on his/her position in the organization.

● EXPERT POWER—In certain cases, subordinates will respond to leaders based on perceptions of the leader's skills, experience or expertise.

● INFORMATION POWER—People with information that is critical to the group gain power through the exclusive possession of this information. However, unlike EXPERT POWER, the power is based on the information, not the person. Once the information becomes available to others, the power is gone.

● REFERENT POWER—Referent power, or charisma, is based on the personality of the leader, again from the perspective of the subordinates. Power is granted based on respect, affection or admiration.

**COMMENT:**
The effectiveness of the use of various sources of power varies with the situation, the leader and the subordinates.

● Reward and coercive power can be applied relatively simply and quickly if organizational rules allow.

● In many informal or volunteer organizations, leaders often have no tangible rewards or punishments at their disposal. Under such conditions, charisma is particularly important.

● While charisma is still a powerful source of power, educated and sophisticated people tend to be reluctant to grant power to others based on personality alone.

# FIGURE 1-10

# BASES

## REFERENT POWER

I CAN LEAP TALL BUILDINGS WITH A SINGLE BOUND.
I HAVE A CUTE CURL IN THE MIDDLE OF MY FOREHEAD
AND I STAND FOR TRUTH, JUSTICE AND THE AMERICAN
WAY. FOLLOW ME!

## COERCIVE POWER

DO WHAT I SAY OR I MAKE
YA AN OFFER YA CAN'T REFUSE.

## INFORMATION POWER    YOU KNOW I'M
THE ONLY ONE WHO KNOWS WHERE THOSE
FILES ARE.  WITHOUT ME, YOU CAN'T DO
ANYTHING.

# OF  POWER

## LEGITIMATE POWER

I OCCUPY THIS BOX AT THE VERY TOP OF THIS
HUGE CONGLOMERATE. I WEAR DARK BLUE
PIN-STRIPE SUITS. MY DESK IS MADE OF
MAHOGANY. MY OFFICE IS HUGE AND I HAVE A
PRIVATE JOHN. FOLLOW ME.

## EXPERT POWER

I AM YOUR TEACHER. I AM
OLD AND WISE. LISTEN TO
ME AND I'LL GIVE YOUR LIVES
MEANING AND SATISFACTION.

## REWARD POWER  AHOY MATEYS.
SHE'S A GALLEON FULL OF GOLD. LET'S TAKE
HER AND WE'LL ALL BE RICH. FOLLOW ME!

- There tends to be an anti-leader syndrome among people in advanced democratic societies. Every time a statue of a leader on a white horse appears, someone seems to send in a flock of pigeons to dump on it. The legitimate right of people to rule as a consequence of their status or position is often questioned. Frequently, leaders must "prove" themselves to their subordinates before they can become fully effective. Recall, if you will, your days in high school when a substitute teacher appeared in the classroom. RAW MEAT! Until that substitute was able to "prove" him/herself, the classroom reflected the discipline of a roller derby.
- The significance of expert power is likely to increase through time in advanced societies where education and knowledge are so critical to effective performance.

## AUTHORITY, ACCOUNTABILITY AND RESPONSIBILITY

Before we leave this introductory chapter, we should address some additional terms associated with leadership and used throughout the book. The focus will be on FORMAL organizations first. Most FORMAL organizations delegate AUTHORITY to make decisions to designated leaders. This AUTHORITY is the *right* of the leader *from the perspective of the organization* to require or prohibit certain actions by subordinates. This right *can* be delegated to subordinates by their leaders.

Such AUTHORITY is inevitably accompanied by ACCOUNTABIL-ITY—the liability owed the organization for performing the leadership task. While some will disagree, I will use the terms, ACCOUNTABILITY and RESPONSIBILITY, interchangeably. Note that ACCOUNTABILITY and RESPONSIBILITY *cannot* be delegated. A leader may make a subordinate responsible *to him/her* for a task, but the leader retains RESPONSIBILITY for all that his/her subordinates do or fail to do.

The RESPONSIBILITY or ACCOUNTABILITY of the leader to the organization is quite clear. However, there is a second dimension to the leader's obligations. Since the leader is influencing the behavior of his/her subordinates, their lives are being affected; the leader *must* assume some RESPONSIBILITY for the welfare of his/her subordinates.

In INFORMAL organizations, the concepts of AUTHORITY, AC-COUNTABILITY and RESPONSIBILITY are more subtle, less defined and subject to the individual interpretations of group members.

**COMMENT:**
Note that, whereas the leader is granted AUTHORITY, he/she becomes ACCOUNTABLE or RESPONSIBLE for the behavior of a group of COMPLEX people who could be extremely unpredictable. Further, the leader becomes ACCOUNTABLE or RESPONSIBLE for events that could

be completely beyond his/her control. Many people recoil from such obligations and prefer to be responsible for their own lives only. Others are lured by the opportunity for AUTHORITY and tend to ignore the accompanying RESPONSIBILITY. They are likely to be ineffective.

A U.S. Army War College study of leadership in the 1970's identified the concept of a "contract" that should exist between leaders and their subordinates. This "contract", usually unwritten, involves the perceptions of the leader and the subordinates of their obligations to one another and to the organization. To the extent that the "contract" is mutually understood and respected, the climate of leadership is likely to be enhanced.[7] This concept of the "contract" is closely related to Chester Barnard's "zone of indifference". According to Barnard, people will accept orders from their bosses so long as they fall within this "zone of indifference", an acceptable range of authority mentally developed by each individual.[8]

**COMMENT:**
When I go into my university classroom with my students, a "contract" of sorts is established. My students will respond without hesitation to prepare a written analysis of a case study I designate (this is part of the learning "contract" in the minds of the students). However, if I ask them to proceed to the faculty parking lot and wash my car (beyond the provisions of the "contract"), they'll ignore me or tell me to get lost. Turning again to the Big Book, we recall the warning "Beware when terms of the 'contract' are not well understood. Ye shall witness loneliness, despair and monumental goof-ups." (Small Paul to the Lebanese Librarians, 66:22.)

## SUMMARY

In this chapter, we discussed the basic steps in the leadership process, four styles of leadership, the sources of power available to the leader and the concepts of authority, accountability, responsibility and the "contract".

Armed with these basic concepts and some definitions, we should now place the leadership task in some perspective. A part of that perspective will be provided in the next chapter, which focuses on evolutionary trends and issues.

## NOTES
[1]Ralph M. Stogdill, *Handbook of Leadership* (New York: The Free Press, 1974), p. 13.

[2]Morgan W. McCall, Jr. and Michael M. Lombardo (Ed.), *Leadership: Where Else Can We Go?* (Durham, NC: Duke University Press, 1978), p. 4.

[3]Tom Peters and Nancy Austin, *A Passion for Excellence* (New York: Random House, 1985), p. xix.

[4]Frederick W. Taylor, *The Principles of Scientific Management* (New York: Harper & Brothers, 1911).

[5]Bernard M. Bass, *Leadership, Psychology and Organizational Behavior* (New York: Harper & Brothers, 1960), p. 90.

[6]John R.P. French and Bertram Raven, "The Bases of Social Power", in Dorwin Cartwright and A.F. Zander (Eds.), *Group Dynamics*, 2d ed. (Evanston, IL: Row, Peterson, 1960), pp. 607-623.

[7]U.S. Army War College, "Leadership in the 1970's", Carlisle Barracks, PA, July 1, 1971.

[8]Chester I. Barnard, *The Functions of the Executive* (Cambridge, MA: Harvard University Press, 1938), pp. 168, 169.

# HOW HAVE ORGANIZATIONS AND THEIR LEADERS CHANGED?

"The number one managerial productivity problem in America is, quite simply, managers who are out of touch with their people and out of touch with their customers."

Tom Peters and Nancy Austin[1]

**COMMENT:**

As I mentioned in the Introduction, I claim that leading people is more demanding and complex than it was in earlier times. This chapter serves to explain why this is the case. Some might object to going back into history—"Forget the historical junk; let's talk about the present." The problem is that times have changed and many people and their organizations haven't adapted. This chapter illustrates how the role and the status of leaders have changed as societies and organizations have become larger, more sophisticated and more interdependent. Developments through time have allowed effective leaders to harness more human energy in organizations than ever before. However, the world is different; the organizations are different; even the people are different. Harnessing that energy—leading effectively—demands more of the leader than ever before. Perhaps the historical perspective that follows will illustrate how and why.

Are you ready to travel? We're about to take a trip; we're going to go back, way back. In just a few minutes of reading, you will be covering centuries of recorded history. We'll be relying on some very "exotic" graphics. We'll be tracing the evolution of organizations and their leaders through time. I'm going to be guilty of some generalizations and omissions in my attempt to make some major points, but please bear with me.

## LEADERS IN ORGANIZATIONS: A HISTORICAL PERSPECTIVE

You should now turn to Figure 2-1 and, for a moment, study its contents. Note that the organization is a triangle operating within an external environment (the display above the triangle). The organization is full of balls. These are people. The location of the ball within the figure (high ball or low ball) and the size of the ball reflect the relative importance and power of the individual. Big, high balls are powerful people. In each case, the big ball at the top of the organization is its leader.

The "distance" measured at the right of the organization reflects the social, economic and psychological distinctions between leaders and the lowest subordinates. The dashed lines indicate "barriers" that tend to prevent people from closing the gap on "distance"—which keep the balls in their "proper" place. Now that we understand the system of graphical representation, let's go back many centuries.

### Prior to the Industrial Revolution

Figure 2-1 reflects a "typical" organization in the environment that existed prior to the Industrial Revolution. Note that the external influences which affect the organization are all static in nature. The focus of governments based on divine right, tradition and religion tends to perpetuate the belief that yesterday, today and tomorrow are likely to be identical. Under such conditions, change is likely to be measured in centuries rather than years. Very few leaders have to cope with profound change. In fact, they become the protectors of the status quo.

Note that the "typical" organization of the time is relatively simple in form and structure. The "walls" of the organization are thick and inflexible—so thick that even the external influences are unlikely to penetrate within the interior of the organization. At the top of the organization is the "great big ball", the leader, with virtually unlimited power over the inner workings of organizational members. The leader's qualifications are a function of his (very rarely her since, at the time, women hardly qualified for ball-dom) blood lines. He could have been as stupid as a pit mule and still qualified as a leader because of the privileges associated with class. Since the functions of the organization are comparatively simple, the leader's supporting staff is relatively small; lines of absolute authority are clear, direct and unambiguous.

Now look down. Note the nature of most of the people in the organization, those who cower in large masses in its lower recesses—A BUNCH OF B-BS! These are people who, because of their status in life,

# FIGURE 2-1

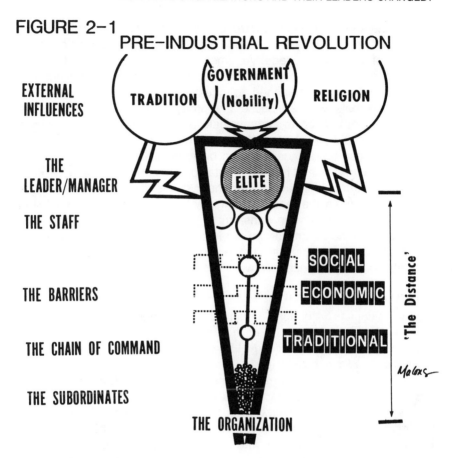

are condemned to a life of thirty years (if they're lucky) of B-B-dom. Their chances of rising to a status of ball-dom are virtually nil because of the pervasiveness of the social, economic and traditional barriers that maintain the status quo. The "distance" between the big ball and his mass of B-Bs is extraordinary. The B-Bs, living very close to the subsistence level and without any power or hope of redress, are at the absolute mercy of the balls.

**COMMENT:**
Not a bad deal at all if you had the good fortune to be born a ball. B-Bs respond pretty readily—they'll even do windows—when power is absolute. Leaders with unquestioned authority could apply coercive power with impunity. Military leaders could offer their B-Bs the chance to "rape and

pillage" the enemy city as a reward for a victorious battle. You know how brutish and irresponsible B-Bs tend to be. Legitimate power was a natural element of the social scene. At times, referent power based on the charisma of the leader could contribute to extraordinary achievements; simple people not conditioned to question could be manipulated by powerful symbols. B-Bs are suckers for pretty faces on white horses. The leader was not obliged to communicate or empathize with the masses very often. Would you really bother to chat with a B-B?

Despite these advantages, it must be recognized that many of these leadership situations that relied on brutal force as the basis for influencing behavior were fragile indeed. When the symbols of that power waned or disappeared, when the leader's banner went down or the leader fell in battle, the scene was often transformed into a leaderless rush to safety with absolutely no regard for the organization. B-Bs often aren't the best of friends when the chips are down. However, better times are ahead; let's refocus our perspective forward to the Industrial Revolution.

## Industrial Revolution—Early Phases

Figure 2-2 depicts a "typical" organization—business or industrial in this case—during the early phases of the Industrial Revolution. At this time, due to opportunities offered by harnessing the sources of power, the development of machines used to manufacture products, and the expansion of markets for these products, people in some nations are flocking from rural areas to the cities to work in factories.

It is important to recognize that the external influences surrounding the organization are beginning to assume more dynamic characteristics. Interest in science, education and exploration is stimulating a grudging willingness to question the past and to change. Such interest in change influences the social scene as people, primarily in Western Europe and America, begin to challenge the privileges of divine right and class systems.

Note that the "typical" organization of the time retains some of the characteristics of its predecessors except that many are becoming bigger and more complex. The "walls" of the organization are less thick, thus reducing the isolation of its members from external influences. The leader is still a "big ball" with tremendous power. In the case of an industrial organization, he (still very rarely she) is an entrepreneur, the owner, decision maker and primary risk-taker of the organization. By this time, the leader needs the assistance of a staff because of the increasing complexity and specialization of organizational operations. Still, the chain of command of the organization is quite clear. Note that some of the social, economic and traditional barriers are just beginning to dissipate.

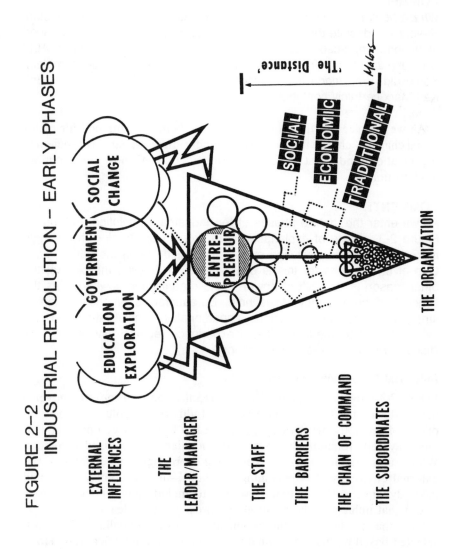

FIGURE 2–2
INDUSTRIAL REVOLUTION – EARLY PHASES

EXTERNAL INFLUENCES

THE LEADER/MANAGER

THE STAFF

THE BARRIERS

THE CHAIN OF COMMAND

THE SUBORDINATES

SOCIAL CHANGE

GOVERNMENT

EDUCATION EXPLORATION

ENTRE-PRENEUR

SOCIAL

ECONOMIC

TRADITIONAL

'The Distance'

THE ORGANIZATION

Despite this, behold the contents of the bottom of the organization—
THEY'RE STILL A BUNCH OF B-Bs! While a few intrepid and lucky
B-Bs are filtering through the barriers to ball-dom, they are the exception.

**COMMENT:**
*What a bummer if you're a B-B!* Despite the achievements of the Industrial
Revolution; despite the fact that goods and services are being produced
at hitherto unprecedented rates, THE BALLS ARE GETTING IT ALL!
Nobody said life is fair, but this is ridiculous. Someone should complain.
Some did. Who made huge noises about the exploitation of the B-Bs?
Karl Marx certainly contributed.

As we can see, portions of the world are being conditioned for major
social change—change that would profoundly affect the nature of societies,
organizations and, most assuredly, their leaders. Let's now move to more
modern times.

**COMMENT:**
As we enter the mature phases of the Industrial Revolution and turn to
Figure 2-3, a note of explanation is in order. I am turning the triangle
representing the organization over—the flat side is on the bottom now.
One of my reasons for this is convenience in drawing the picture; the
other reason is the shift of power in the organization downward as the
concept of bureaucracy takes hold. Bureaucracies emphasize formal
structures, rules and regulations, impersonality, specialization and promotion based on merit (merit and experience replace "divine right" as
"tickets" to success—at least in theory).

**Industrial Revolution—Mature Phases**

Figure 2-3 depicts a "typical" large organization—business or government—during the mature phases of the Industrial Revolution. The simplicity of previous structures is gone and has been replaced by complex,
multi-layered, functionally organized and highly specialized elements.
While such organizations are becoming more rigid and inflexible, the
external environment is beginning to "boil"—it is becoming more and
more dynamic with additional groups, to include government, gaining
power that influences the position and prestige of the leader.

Note that the leader of the organization, still a big ball, is a steward,
selected based on his (occasionally her) managerial qualifications. However, the leader's power is often shared with groups such as the owners
or shareholders of the organization. The leader is assisted by an extraordinary bevy of line and staff subordinates to coordinate the complex
operations of the bureaucratic behemoth. Note that some of the barriers

# FIGURE 2-3
## INDUSTRIAL REVOLUTION – MATURE PHASES

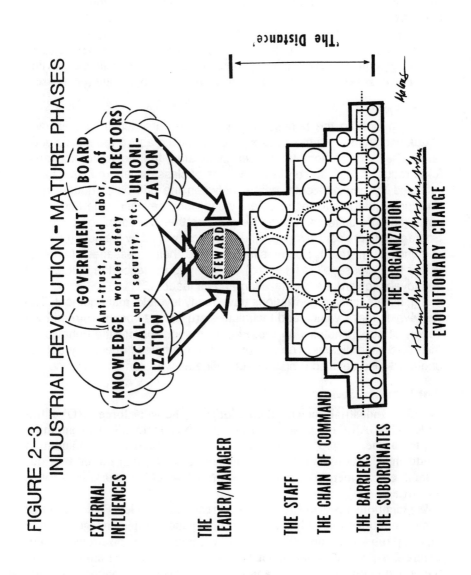

EXTERNAL
INFLUENCES

THE
LEADER/MANAGER

THE STAFF

THE CHAIN OF COMMAND

THE BARRIERS
THE SUBORDINATES

have switched from horizontal to vertical orientations. These are barriers associated with specialization that will be discussed later.

Most profound, however, observe the developments in the bottom of the organization. At long last, the B-Bs have "graduated"—they've achieved the exalted status of GOLF BALLS! Further, the "distance" between the golf balls and the bigger balls up the line is shrinking. To make matters "worse", some of those golf balls have the nerve to join unions. A bunch of golf balls together in a bag can look like a bowling ball. Power is beginning to be distributed to many to include the masses.

## COMMENT:

Finally, people in the bottom of organizations are acquiring their own status and "rights". In most cases, they are living above the subsistence level. Their expectations have been stimulated; their tolerance for brute force reduced. Still, some of the vestiges of class society remain. One is reflected by one horizontal barrier between the golf balls (bottom row) and those just above them. Often, distinctions between blue and white collar jobs are quite pervasive. We can see the "put down" on paydays. Some people are paid salaries; others are paid wages by the hour (obvious evidence of mistrust). Such distinctions and their "messages" (whether or not the "message" is intended) are likely to influence the attitudes of employees toward the organization and its leaders.

Big, bureaucratic organizations have many levels of management. The top-level leader's values and techniques are going to be interpreted by a variety of subordinates who are, in turn, responsible for the behavior of their own subordinates. The leader must not only lead effectively but he/she must also develop a host of subordinates who can do the same.

### Post-Industrial Society

In a Post-Industrial Society, the majority of the work force PROVIDES SERVICES AS OPPOSED TO PRODUCING THINGS. This situation exists in the United States today. We have become so efficient at producing things (or our foreign competitors have) that the bulk of our gainful employment is associated with white collar work or service industries.

We mentioned previously that the bureaucratic model (Figure 2-3) had some limitations—notably the ability to respond to rapid change. Despite this limitation, there are still plenty of bureaucratic organizations around. Figure 2-4 portrays what might be considered a modern alternative to the bureaucratic organization appropriate for firms in dynamic, changing situations.

Organizations designed to respond to change are flexible, not rigid. Under such conditions, our "typical" organization resembles an expand-

## FIGURE 2–4

## POST–INDUSTRIAL SOCIETY

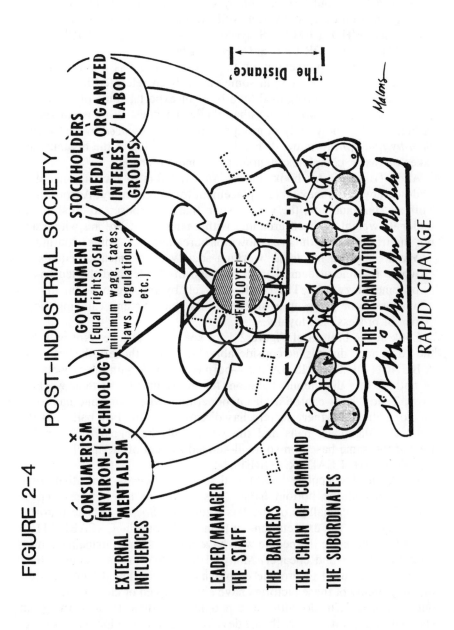

EXTERNAL
INFLUENCES

LEADER/MANAGER
THE STAFF

THE BARRIERS

THE CHAIN OF COMMAND

THE SUBORDINATES

RAPID CHANGE

ing and contracting bag with membrane-like walls that allow for frequent penetrations and out-oozings. Many of the dynamic forces external to the organization enter at a variety of locations completely circumventing the leader WHO REMAINS RESPONSIBLE FOR EVERYTHING THAT HAPPENS OR FAILS TO HAPPEN.

Note that the complexion of the organization has changed rather drastically. The leader has, in some cases, been relegated to the status of an "employee" surrounded by a bevy of experts, some of whom are smarter and make more money than the leader does. What is not shown in Figure 2-4 is the variety of groups of people, *organized by task rather than by function*, forming, disbanding and reforming as the organization takes on tasks, completes them and responds to change.

Alvin Toffler, in his book, *Future Shock*, refers to such a concept as "ad-hocracy", the inevitable replacement for bureaucracy. According to Toffler, "bureaucracy, the very system that is supposed to crush us all under its weight, is itself groaning with change. . . . We are witnessing not the triumph, but the breakdown of bureaucracy." Toffler continues,

We are moving toward a 'working society of technical co-equals' where the line of demarkation between the leader and the led has become fuzzy. . . . The old loyalty felt by the organization man appears to be going up in smoke. In its place we are watching the rise of professional loyalty.[2]

Look at the bottom of Figure 2-4 for some real change. Not only has the "distance" diminished considerably, but look at those at the bottom— A BUNCH OF TENNIS BALLS—born tennis balls with the expectation of nothing less than tennis ball-dom for the remainder of their working lives. Tennis balls can be a bit uncooperative when someone has to go out for coffee. Further, society has directed that the boy balls and the girl balls, the black balls and the white balls be mixed together and treated the same based on some ill-defined system of merit WHETHER OR NOT THE LEADER AGREES!

The leader has acquired additional social challenges. Note that some of the balls at the bottom have "pits" (dots at the bottom). These symbolize the casualties of the Post-Industrial Society—those unfortunates who have the expectations of tennis balls but the CAPABILITIES OF B-Bs! These are the people who have no skills that a machine cannot do better, faster and cheaper. Many of them live in inner cities where large factories used to provide employment for unskilled labor. Unfortunately, many of these factories have either moved or closed down. The question is what to do with these people—pay them to do nothing but stay out of the way? ignore them? develop them into productive workers? Does this affect the business leader? Definitely. Many people in today's society are urging today's business leaders to divert profits (normally distributed to shareholders) and improvements to tend to the needs of these people. Some respond that this is properly the function of government. However, these are often the same people who oppose large government. Business leaders find themselves "in the middle". The "traditional" and relatively simple objective of the business leader— profit maximization—is challenged by others involving social welfare.

**COMMENT:**
If Figure 2-4 is considered at least generally representative, it is clear that some of today's leaders operate within an environment that combines the characteristics of a Roman orgy, a demolition derby and a three-ring circus. The organization has become a bewildering array of vaguely structured temporary groups. The power of the leader, once virtually absolute, has become diffused and shared with many to include those at the very bottom of the organization. Further, forces external to the organization have the ability to distract, confuse or alienate its members. Despite this, it remains the role of the leader to harness the resources and to create the environment within which members will willingly "bend their arrows" to achieve group objectives. Finally, in a dynamic environment, the "arrow bending" process never ends; tasks and objectives are continually changing. The effective leader must be adept at determining "which way to go".

# CONTEMPORARY TRENDS AND ISSUES THAT INFLUENCE THE LEADER

While the historical overview, just discussed, identified developments which influence the leader, some deserve further elaboration and explanation.

### The Loss of Power

Figure 2-5 illustrates the "traditional" status of the leader with regard to raw power—the ability to obtain dominance over others. The leader was "armed"; his/her subordinates were not. This situation was often unquestioned and tolerated as "natural" and "right" based on the social conditioning of the class system. Whereas the leader could be thoughtful and benevolent if he/she liked, the six-gun, symbolic of coercive power, tended to be quicker and more effective—it was used frequently.

Figure 2-6 depicts a somewhat different situation, perhaps exaggerated, but representative of the "arms race" that has occurred in modern societies and their organizations. In this case, the leader's arsenal of raw power has been reduced to one six-gun. More important, however, the leader now operates within an "armed camp". He/she can be "blown away" by a group or groups that never before had significant power. The

# FIGURE 2-5 POWER OF THE LEADER THEN

# FIGURE 2-6    POWER OF THE LEADER NOW

leader can still pull his/her six-gun and use force, but such actions should now be reserved for emergencies. The leader had better develop some of the qualities of a lion tamer rather than those of a ruthless tyrant. Powers of persuasion become important. Many who can't take such odds would rather go off and smell the flowers than take on the responsibilities of influencing the behavior of others who now have the ability to make the leader's life miserable.

**COMMENT:**
The subject of redistribution of power can take on many dimensions. We've said that leaders need power in order to operate; that powerful people get respect. Nowadays, it isn't all that simple. Raw power can attract a lot of animosity and hate. Take the case of the super-powers, the U.S. and the Soviet Union. Either can literally blow the world away. However, they can't rationally use such power. They have become so powerful that, in some respects, they can't accomplish much without dire consequences. Meanwhile, they catch a lot of "flack" from the little balls who resent their size and blame them for a multitude of evils. Big balls are big targets. Sensing this, many go to considerable efforts to conceal their size. Others try very hard to be popular. This brings up a good question; does a leader need to be *popular* with subordinates in order to be effective?

Meanwhile, technology has allowed some tiny balls to use power and, in the process, get a lot of instant publicity. Consider the power of a demented B-B with a bomb aboard a fully-loaded commercial air liner. We live in a fragile world with a desperate need for cool heads.

### The Explosion of Knowledge
Figure 2-7 illustrates the status of Man when the "pile" of accumulated knowledge was relatively small. During these traditional times, one man (rarely a woman—it wasn't in style) could "hunker down" on all of the knowledge necessary to become an "expert" and run an organization. With such expertise, this individual could make all of the significant decisions single-handedly—very little consultation with others was needed.

Figure 2-8 portrays the tremendous change in the "pile of knowledge" that has occurred since the Industrial Revolution. Ours has become a "knowledge society" where knowledge and the ability to apply it have become tantamount to power.

What happens to people who seek a "place in the sun" under such conditions? Figure 2-9 illustrates this. They specialize. Recognizing that they cannot "swallow" the whole pile, they seek a "hunk" that appeals to them and dig. They dig deep but very narrow holes; they become "experts" in very limited areas. Sensing a need to affiliate with others,

# FIGURE 2-7

# KNOWLEDGE THEN

## MAN, THE "EXPERT"

## AVAILABLE KNOWLEDGE

# WHEN LIFE WAS SIMPLE

FIGURE 2-8

## KNOWLEDGE NOW

FIGURE 2-9

## SPECIALIZATION AND EXCLUSIVITY

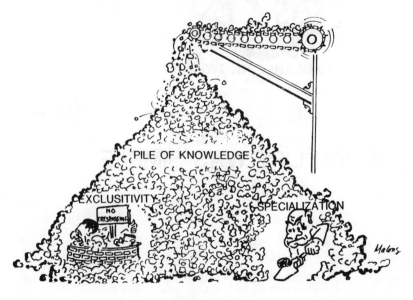

they look for others with the same specialty and share the same hole. Seeking some degree of uniqueness or identity, they build walls around their holes to keep out the "unworthy"—those who do not share their specialty. They do this in both overt and subtle ways. Sometimes they form professional societies. Almost always, they develop a special language that only those in the hole understand. Thus, they acquire INFORMATION POWER and EXPERT POWER (Chapter One). This makes them feel good.

Very often, leaders who are responsible for the performance of many people in many widely diverse holes—WHO NEED ALL OF THEIR KNOWLEDGE IN ORDER TO MAKE DECISIONS—are "outsiders". After all, there's just so much they can learn during a lifetime.

## COMMENT:

No longer can today's leaders of organizations involving any size or complexity rely solely on their own knowledge, experience, expertise or intuition. In order to make interdisciplinary decisions (decisions requiring inputs from a variety of specialties—most significant decisions do), they MUST rely on the expertise and judgments of others. This involves a further redistribution of power *away* from the leader. This requires that the leader become adept at identifying, selecting and developing the loyalty of a bunch of "hole diggers" who have knowledge the leader needs.

Further, the leader should seek a "decoder" for the many languages developed by the specialists—in essence, a MEGALANGUAGE. This language should incorporate all of the specialized languages and be totally devoid of subjectivity. Which language is that? It's the LANGUAGE OF NUMBERS. What speaks the language of numbers? THE COMPUTER. The megalanguage of organizations is numbers; the computer, the supreme number-cruncher, is the storehouse of information; those who tend the computer preside over a critical resource in the "knowledge society". Who are they? COMPUTER WEENIES. They are powerful people. Remember the words of the Big Book, "Take a computer weenie to lunch!" (Small Paul to the Digitalizers, 22:47.)

### The Increasing Complexity of People

Chapter Three will go into some detail about human motivation and what makes people do what they do. This will include an examination of Abraham Maslow's famous hierarchy of needs that is portrayed in Figure 2-10. What is becoming increasingly apparent is the fact that, as people's relatively predictable lower-level (physiological and security) needs are being satisfied, more sophisticated needs are being uncovered. When this occurs, human behavior becomes more complicated and unpredictcable.

# FIGURE 2–10

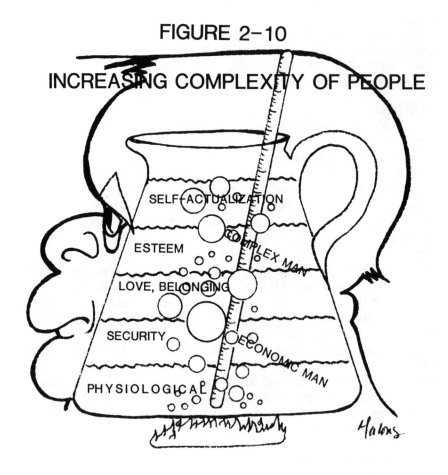

INCREASING COMPLEXITY OF PEOPLE

People aren't basically different; we're just discovering new things about them as they adapt to affluence and life styles hitherto considered unattainable. In the Industrial Revolution, we gave them plenty of THINGS; now they're seeking "quality of life", whatever that is. In many cases, they're seeking this quality in the workplace and they're expecting their leaders to provide it. Their expectations are high. Tennis balls can be quite a bother; they expect far more attention than B-Bs. They yell "foul" and "love" and expect busy leaders to give them strokes. James Cribbin describes their characteristics as follows:

- Changing people think.
- Changing people are no longer meek.
- Changing people are self-interested.
- Changing people expect to be heard.
- Changing people are more expensive than ever.
- Changing people have great potential.[3]

### Discoveries about Organizations

Concern about the apparent ineffectiveness of "traditional" organizations—PARTICULARLY THEIR INABILITY TO ADAPT TO CHANGE—has led to significant discoveries about their basic natures. One of these is portrayed in Figure 2-11. The organization is compared to an iceberg. The formal and readily observable aspects of the organization (those above the waterline) are naturally significant. In the past, they have been the focus of attempts to "fix" the organization when trouble occurred. Many of these attempts amounted to band-aid approaches—the "disease" was never identified. Further investigation revealed that the real "essence" of the organization lay below the waterline. This includes the attitudes, values, expectations and goals of organizational members individually and in their INFORMAL GROUPS. Interest was stimulated in the "organizational culture" and its effects on people. While some "below the waterline" therapy has been unsuccessful (it goes by a variety of names to include Organizational Development), it has contributed to an enhanced ability to detect and reduce organizational problems.

## COMMENT:

Today's leaders must be able to develop a sensitivity to what's going on "below the waterline". They must develop access to information, TO INCLUDE THE BAD NEWS, concerning the attitudes, values, expectations and goals of subordinates. They must understand that human beings behave both rationally and emotionally, and that both aspects can be productive. They must "learn to balance the material wonders of technology with the spiritual demands of our human nature."[4]

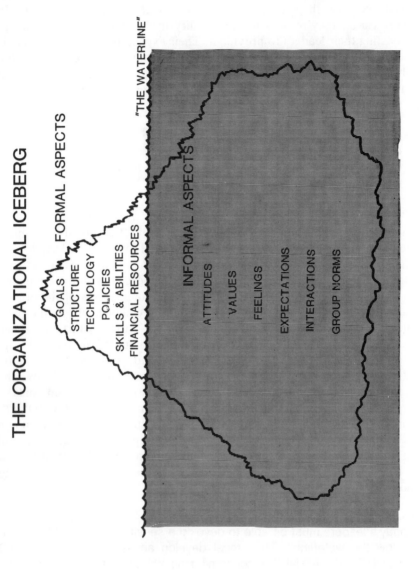

FIGURE 2–11

THE ORGANIZATIONAL ICEBERG

FORMAL ASPECTS

GOALS
STRUCTURE
TECHNOLOGY
POLICIES
SKILLS & ABILITIES
FINANCIAL RESOURCES

"THE WATERLINE"

INFORMAL ASPECTS

ATTITUDES
VALUES
FEELINGS
EXPECTATIONS
INTERACTIONS
GROUP NORMS

### The Leader's New Role and Status

A primary role of the leader in a tradition-bound society was the preservation of the status quo. Very few organizations in a Post-Industrial Society thrive on the status quo despite the fact that many people value normalcy and security very highly. Many of today's leaders must serve as the organization's "engine of change"—influencing the behavior of subordinates, many of them recalcitrant, toward "better" things. This can be tough. Machiavelli warned, "There is nothing more difficult to take in hand, more perilous to conduct, or more uncertain in its success, than to take the lead in the introduction of new things."[5] Making changes when power was concentrated was tough; now power is widely shared. There is no question that PARTICIPATION IS IN—DECISION MAKING MUST BE SHARED WITH OTHERS. The "distance" between the leader and the subordinates has been reduced by society. The leader must be many things to many people. The question is HOW. The HOW will be developed in the chapters which follow.

### COMMENT:

No longer can the leader lounge back in splendid isolation and expect the B-Bs to bow and scrape. As predicted in the Big Book, "No longer can the leader expect subordinates to soar with the eagles while he/she slops with the hogs" (Small Paul to the Philanderers, 73:14). The "distance" has contracted; nowadays, what's good for the boss is perceived as justified for the subordinate. Leaders who set poor examples get a lot of attention and do a lot of harm.

## SUMMARY

In this chapter, we have traced the evolution of leaders and their organizations through history highlighting trends and developments that must be recognized in order to be effective in today's environment. The resources available to accomplish things through collective human effort have never been greater; the challenges associated with harnessing those energies also have never been greater. Despite the challenges, the need for effective leadership is very real.

It is the paradox of our times that precisely when the trust and credibility of our leaders are at their lowest, when the beleaguered survivors in leadership positions feel unable to summon up the vestiges of power left to them, we most need people who can lead.[6]

## NOTES

[1]Tom Peters and Nancy Austin, *A Passion for Excellence* (New York: Random House, 1985), p. 8.

[2]Alvin Toffler, *Future Shock* (New York: Random House, Inc., 1970), pp. 125, 142, 146.

[3]James J. Cribbin, *Leadership: Strategies for Organizational Effectiveness* (New York: AMACOM, 1981), pp. 2, 3.

[4]John Naisbitt, *Megatrends* (New York: Warner Books, Inc., 1982), p. 40.

[5]Bernard M. Bass, *Leadership, Psychology and Organizational Behavior* (New York: Harper & Brothers, 1960), p. 83.

[6]Warren Bennis, *The Unconscious Conspiracy: Why Leaders Can't Lead* (New York: AMACOM, 1976), p. 157.

# CHAPTER THREE

# WHAT TURNS PEOPLE ON AND OFF?

"We can no longer expect a single motivation scheme, punishment system, or communication style to produce the same results for all employees. We must develop customized approaches in tune with the value systems of each sub-group of employees."

Morris Massey[1]

Why is this chapter necessary? In our definition of leadership—GETTING PEOPLE TO DO THINGS—WILLINGLY—two key words stand out—PEOPLE and THINGS. In this chapter we will examine the PEOPLE. We're going to hit a few high points only, recognizing that Man's knowledge of people literally fills countless volumes. We're going to focus on motivation or the WHY of human behavior. Why such a focus? As a leader, your role is to influence the behavior of others. YOUR behavior will be influenced by YOUR interpretations of why your subordinates think and behave as they do.

**COMMENT:**
Let's take the example of Hugo, your 170-pound English sheep dog with the black tongue and one red eye (remember that dogs are much simpler than COMPLEX people). You have just purchased wall-to-wall carpeting. To your chagrin, Hugo has made substantial unhygienic deposits on your investment several times. After some very emotional episodes, Hugo has ceased his unsportsmanlike behavior, at least temporarily. You would like to know WHY so you can continue to protect the rug. You have narrowed Hugo's reasons for cooperating to the following:
- Hugo admires and respects you and wants to keep your love.
- Hugo prefers to potty outside.
- Hugo recalls the last time he went on the rug when you hit him between the eyes with a brick.

- None of these.
- All of these.

Based on your analysis, you will either (a) pet him a lot, (b) keep the outside door open, (c) carry a large brick in your pocket, (d) sell Hugo or (e) live with a smelly rug. YOUR behavior has been conditioned by YOUR analysis of WHY Hugo behaves as he does.

But enough about dogs and such potty talk; let's turn back to people. They're more unpredictable, and no two of them view the world identically because they're COMPLEX.

**COMMENT:**
Let's see if we can develop the ability to EMPATHIZE—to view the world from the perspectives of others—and thus be able to anticipate their actions and reactions. For some potential leaders, this requires a shift of personal orientation from exclusive interest in "ME" to a genuine concern for "WE". Some people find such a shift impossible. In my opinion, they should, for the benefit of all, discontinue their interest in leading and seek some other activity.

## WHAT IS HUMAN MOTIVATION?

Motivation refers to the causes or the WHY of behavior. However, there is a problem. The problem is that motivation cannot be measured directly. It cannot be seen or felt but can only be inferred based on observations of behavior. Motivation is an illusive concept, but it does involve a burst or bursts of energy. Let us, for the purpose of clarity and simplicity, refer to it as an "inner spark"—a spark that stimulates action on the part of the "sparker"—some human being.

**COMMENT:**
Based on the description, above, is it logical to conclude that it is the role of the leader to *motivate subordinates* to achieve the objectives of the organization? *ABSOLUTELY NOT!* There's the rub! Motivation is an INNER drive or spark. THE ONLY PERSON YOU CAN MOTIVATE IS YOURSELF. The leader influences the behavior of subordinates *indirectly* through the organizational environment he/she creates. Subordinates interpret the "signals" personally and individually. Their actions and reactions can vary. (See Figure 3-1)

Many authors write of "motivating subordinates" and classify motivation as one of the functions of management and leadership. I consider them somewhat "misguided", but they have published widely and I have not, so I will hush up.

FIGURE 3–1

SURE, EVERYONE IS MOTIVATED, BUT. . .

Before we turn to some theoretical approaches concerning motivation, let's clarify a few points. Abraham Maslow noted that "Man is a wanting animal". His message is that people are always wanting something; their spark generators are ALWAYS cranking; they're always looking for something else; they're NEVER fully satisfied. When they quit generating sparks; when they're completely satisfied, THEY'RE DEAD. According to Maslow, everyone is motivated to do SOMETHING. However, for our purposes, we must refer back to our definition of a "motivated subordinate"—*one who is committed to IMPROVING performance*. Of course, the performance we're interested in contributes to the organization.

Most healthy people keep an untapped reservoir of potential energy (reserve sparks) for special occasions. It would be great if leaders could create conditions where subordinates would not only generate sparks in directions useful to the organization, BUT ALSO reach down and commit their reserves. An understanding of what makes people tick may help in achieving this.

## McGREGOR'S THEORY X AND THEORY Y

Unfortunately, there isn't much agreement concerning how people tick. Douglas McGregor highlighted the extent of disagreement with his famous Theory X and Theory Y views of Man. These constitute EXTREME assumptions about people and their attitudes toward work; the assumptions of most people lie somewhere between these two extremes.

Theory X, considered the "traditional view" (perhaps associated with B-Bs), is based on an extremely pessimistic perspective of people:

### THEORY X ASSUMPTIONS

● The average person has an inherent dislike for work and will avoid it if he or she can.

● Because of this human characteristic of dislike of work, most people must be coerced, controlled, directed and threatened with punishment to get them to put forth adequate effort toward the achievement of organizational objectives.

● The average person prefers to be directed, wishes to avoid responsibility, has relatively little ambition, and wants security above all.

Theory Y, the other extreme, is a more optimistic and modern view (perhaps associated with golf or tennis balls). Theory Y assumptions are listed below:

### THEORY Y ASSUMPTIONS

● The expenditure of physical and mental effort in work is as natural as play or rest.

● People will exercise self-direction and self-control in the service of objectives to which they are committed.

48

FIGURE 3-2
McGREGOR'S EXTREME VIEWPOINTS OF MAN

THEORY X

I HATE WORK.
IF YOU HIRE ME, YOU'D BETTER
WATCH ME CLOSELY.
DON'T YOU DARE GIVE ME ANY
RESPONSIBILITY.

THEORY Y

I FIND WORK AS NATURAL AS
PLAY AND REST.
JUST TELL ME WHAT YOU WANT
DONE. I'LL FIGURE OUT HOW TO
DO IT. I WANT RESPONSIBILITY.
I CAN BE CREATIVE.

• Commitment to objectives is a function of the rewards associated with achievement.

• The average person learns, under proper conditions, not only to accept but also to seek responsibility.

• The capacity to exercise a relatively high degree of imagination, ingenuity and creativity in the solution of organizational problems is widely, not narrowly, distributed in the population.[2]

McGregor implied that the Theory Y approach contributes to better results in most cases. He noted that the leader's assumptions about subordinates will influence the leader's behavior and, in turn, the subordinates' behavior. People who are treated in a "Theory X manner" are likely to respond according to the Theory X description of people— a case of the "self-fulfilling prophecy".

**COMMENT:**
Consider the case of Aaron Aardvark who took over Optimo Optics when the previous boss retired. The entire work force at Optimo was particularly motivated. People knew their jobs and worked well without supervision. Further, they were full of ideas concerning how to improve performance. They resembled "Theory Y people" very closely.

However, Aaron believed deep down in his heart that most people were basically lazy. With this in mind, he insisted on making all of the decisions, he set up strict controls, he checked on everything and everyone and he ignored the suggestions of subordinates. Pretty soon they got the message. "If I'm going to be treated like a lazy lout, I might as well act like one". The subordinates modified their behavior to conform to the expectations of their boss; the "self-fulfilling prophecy" came true.

# CHRIS ARGYRIS' MATURITY/IMMATURITY CONTINUUM

Chris Argyris studied the effects of the maturing process on human beings and developed his Maturity/Immaturity Continuum. Argyris observed that, as most people mature, they move:

• From a state of passivity as an infant to a state of increasing activity as an adult.

• From a state of dependence on others as an infant to a state of relative independence as an adult.

• From a state of behaving only in a few ways as an infant to being capable of behaving in many different ways as an adult.

• From having erratic, casual, shallow and quickly dropped interests as an infant to having deeper interests as an adult.

• From having a short time perspective as an infant to having a much longer time perspective as an adult.

FIGURE 3–3

MATURITY–IMMATURITY CONTINUUM

MAN'S DEVELOPMENT FROM INFANCY
TO MATURITY AND CREATIVITY

- From a lack of awareness of self as an infant to awareness and control over self as an adult.[3]

**COMMENT:**
Most mature adults, who value their uniqueness and freedom, realize that they must sacrifice some of this in order to conform to the restrictions of the working environment in accordance with some form of "contract". A "contract" which includes provisions which appear childish to subordinates may literally "turn them off". If they are forced to accept such a situation, it is very likely that they will "bank their sparks" at work and save them for more mature pursuits well beyond the workplace.

Take, for example, conditions at the Humongous Housewares. All activities of employees—coffee and rest room breaks, lunch breaks, the beginning and the end of the work day—are controlled by buzzers and bells. Deviations from the regular routine are not tolerated. Mature employees are likely to view such control measures as "kids' stuff" and resent them deeply. Their resentment could be expressed in various forms of childish behavior such as jokes, pranks and games with management as the "victims"—"If they're gonna treat me like a kid, I'll bloody well act like one".

Some leaders use a style of leadership that is classified as BENEVO-LENT AUTHORITATIVE. The benevolent authoritative leader treats his/her subordinates with kindness and consideration—like children—but makes all of the decisions. B-Bs might consider this better than working for a true animal, but golf balls, and particularly tennis balls, are likely to demand more respect and mature treatment.

## ABRAHAM MASLOW'S NEEDS-GOALS APPROACH

Abraham Maslow is world famous for his NEEDS-GOALS approach to human motivation. Simply stated, Maslow's theory has three components:

- Man is a wanting animal—he/she is always wanting something. Hence, motivation is a continuous process; as one need is satisfied, another arises.

- Man is not motivated by a satisfied need. Once a particular need is satisfied, his/her behavior is influenced by another UNSATISFIED need.

- Man's basic needs can be arranged in a hierarchy of importance or order in which individuals generally strive to satisfy them. Usually, the lower-level needs are stronger and are satisfied first; then the individual "looks up" the hierarchy to satisfy the higher-level needs. The needs are described below, starting from the most basic need to the higher-level needs.

PHYSIOLOGICAL—includes the need for air, water, food, shelter and sex.

SECURITY—includes the need for safety, order and freedom from fear or threat.

BELONGINGNESS AND LOVE (or social need)—includes the need for love, affection, feelings of belonging and social contact.

ESTEEM—includes the need for self-respect, self-esteem, achievement and respect from others.

SELF-ACTUALIZATION—includes the need to grow, to feel fulfilled and to realize one's full potential.[4]

## COMMENT:

Maslow says that, if we want people to generate big sparks, we should (a) determine what level of needs are satisfied AND THEN (b) LOOK UP to the next higher level of the hierarchy. For example, if a person's physiological and security needs are *essentially* satisfied, LOOK UP, give the bloke some *love*, provide a working environment that satisfies his *social* needs.

On the surface, this seems simple. Practically, speaking, there are many complications. It is acknowledged that most needs are not COM-PLETELY satisfied—it's not like a pitcher of water where you "fill" physiological completely and then begin to "fill" security. Further, people are likely to "bounce around" the hierarchy. A person who is literally glowing with self-actualization (the top-level need) can very quickly zoom down to his security needs if a thug shoves a pistol up his nose. Finally, Maslow's model portrays Man as a consummate "wanter" or "taker". Some very powerful human motivation based on GIVING—giving of time, dedication, even life—is not explained by Maslow's theory. We may never know precisely what motivated the man or woman who drove the explosive-laden truck into the U.S. Marine compound in Beirut and caused so many deaths.

Despite its limitations, Maslow's theory helps to explain why certain attempts to stimulate human motivation have failed. People who perceive that they earn sufficient money are unlikely to WORK HARDER for more money—they might value the extra time to spend their money far more highly. An auto worker with a good income might feel a real need for a three-day weekend that he can readily afford. If the boss won't grant it, he might take it anyway. Here we witness absenteeism in action—a vital link in the assembly of an automobile is missing. The chance that a defective machine will be produced is enhanced.

As people climb Maslow's hierarchy, they enter the more complex areas of human behavior. The leader's job of empathizing with subordinates and predicting their behavior becomes more complicated; the chances of error increase.

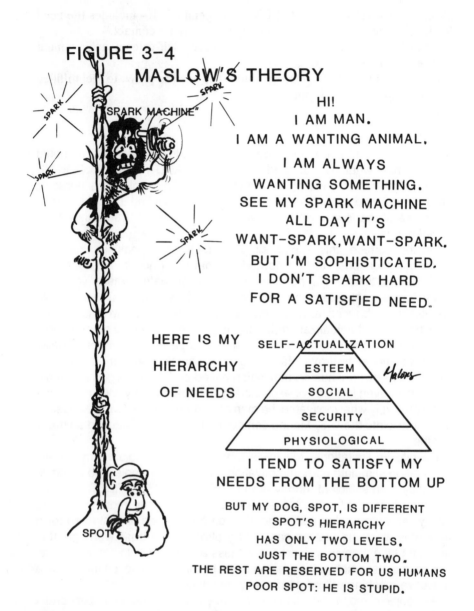

FIGURE 3-4
MASLOW'S THEORY

# ANOTHER VIEW OF HUMAN NEEDS

David McClellan, among others, has approached the study of human motivation based on a different set of needs. These needs are ACHIEVE-MENT, AFFILIATION and POWER. People are different with regard to the intensity of these needs. In most cases, experiences early in their lives have determined these intensities. For example, children of high-achieving parents are quite likely to have strong needs for achievement—a result of values acquired at home during childhood. As will be discussed later, effective leaders are likely to have strong needs for POWER.[5]

**COMMENT:**
Here we go muddying the water with an entirely new set of "needs". Maslow had his and now here comes McClellan. But wait; there's more to come.

# FREDERICK HERZBERG'S TWO FACTOR THEORY OF MOTIVATION

Based on extensive research with a variety of groups in several working environments (blue collar, white collar, professionals), Frederick Herzberg developed a "Two Factor Theory of Motivation". Herzberg and his associates asked the subjects of his experiments to think of times when they felt especially BAD and especially GOOD about their working environments. The responses were remarkably consistent.

With regard to the BAD responses, those factors that contributed to DISSATISFACTION, the following were prominent:
- Company policy and administration
- Technical supervision
- Interpersonal relations with supervisors, peers and subordinates
- Salary
- Job security
- Personal life
- Work conditions
- Status

Herzberg classified these as HYGIENE or MAINTENANCE FACTORS, or potential sources of dissatisfaction. Note that they all relate to the CONTEXT of the working environment.

With regard to the conditions that made people feel GOOD about their jobs, the following were prominent among responses:
- Achievement
- Recognition
- Advancement
- The work itself

- The possibility of personal growth
- Responsibility

Herzberg classified these as satisfiers or MOTIVATORS. Note that they all relate to the CONTENT of the job.

Herzberg then applied these observations to develop his two factor theory, which conflicts with the traditional view of employee satisfaction. According to the traditional view, there is a continuum between complete satisfaction and complete dissatisfaction. (See Figure 3-5.) Herzberg disagrees. According to Herzberg, employees can range from complete dissatisfaction to a "neutral" state or absence of dissatisfaction BASED ON CONDITIONS ASSOCIATED WITH THE HYGIENE OR MAINTENANCE FACTORS. However, according to Herzberg, these people would NOT be motivated or satisfied—they would simply be without dissatisfaction. Satisfaction and, in turn, motivation occur only when the other factors, the MOTIVATORS, are applied.[6]

**COMMENT:**

What does Herzberg's theory mean to the leader? If Herzberg is correct, developing an organizational climate conducive to subordinate motivation (committed to improving performance) involves TWO, not one, steps:

- FIRST—Reduce the dissatisfaction by focusing on the HYGIENE factors (this produces "neutral" people—neither dissatisfied nor motivated).
- THEN—focus on the MOTIVATORS.

Note that *step one is an essential precondition for step two*. Herzberg's research led to considerable interest in the concept of JOB ENRICHMENT, adding more responsibility to the job (one of the MOTIVATORS). Job enrichment will be addressed in detail later in this chapter.

It is interesting to note that Herzberg's theory was apparently applied in the 1970s when conscription in the U.S. was terminated and the Armed Forces had to compete in the labor market for volunteers. FIRST, inequities among HYGIENE factors such as pay, working conditions and status were addressed. THEN, considerable attention was focused on conditions associated with the work itself—the MOTIVATORS.

Before we leave Herzberg, two terms that will come up later should be introduced—INTRINSIC and EXTRINSIC rewards. INTRINSIC rewards are part of the job and occur *when the employee performs the work*. Note that Herzberg's MOTIVATORS are all INTRINSIC in nature. EXTRINSIC rewards are external rewards that have meaning or value AFTER the work has been performed or away from the workplace. Note that some, not all, of Herzberg's HYGIENE factors are EXTRINSIC in nature. Pay is a classic example of an EXTRINSIC reward; the money

FIGURE 3-5

HERZBERG'S TWO FACTOR THEORY

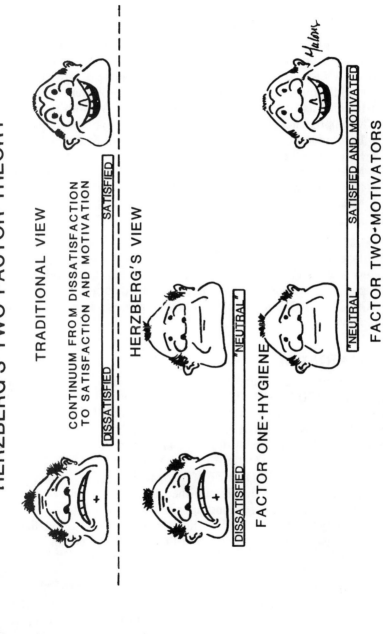

TRADITIONAL VIEW

CONTINUUM FROM DISSATISFACTION
TO SATISFACTION AND MOTIVATION

DISSATISFIED ——————————— SATISFIED

HERZBERG'S VIEW

DISSATISFIED ——————— "NEUTRAL"

FACTOR ONE-HYGIENE

"NEUTRAL" ——————— SATISFIED AND MOTIVATED

FACTOR TWO-MOTIVATORS

is spent and presumably enjoyed away from the workplace after the work is done.

## AND THERE ARE MORE

We have just scratched the surface of research and writing on motivation that focuses on the NEEDS-GOALS approach. Some eminent theorists such as Victor Vroom, Lyman Porter and Edward Lawler have gone beyond Maslow and attempted to relate the achievement of a goal to the satisfactions associated with that achievement. We won't go into detail on their approaches. However, we should remember the following advice:
- Determine the rewards valued by each subordinate.
- Determine the performance you desire.
- Make the performance level attainable.
- Link rewards to performance.
- Make sure the reward is adequate.[7]

**COMMENT:**
The leader faces somewhat of a dilemma if the rewards valued by a variety of subordinates are inconsistent. How can the leader be fair and impartial and, at the same time, recognize the differences among people? GOOD QUESTION! If you plan to reward inconsistently, be prepared to explain WHY.

## BEHAVIORISM

B.F. Skinner is a particularly prominent researcher and writer who represents BEHAVIORISM. According to the behaviorists, the CONSEQUENCES of behavior, NOT ANY SUPPOSED INNER MENTAL OR EMOTIONAL PROCESS, determine the ways people behave. Essentially, the inner needs of people are disregarded. Instead, the focus is upon BEHAVIOR MODIFICATION and the LAW OF EFFECT. According to the LAW OF EFFECT, behavior that is rewarded tends to be repeated; behavior that is punished tends to be eliminated. We see many applications of behavioral approaches in education.

According to behavior modification theory, the key to "getting people to do things—willingly" is ensuring that desired behavior is rewarded. People learn proper behavior by repeated rewards or POSITIVE REINFORCEMENTS.

Behaviorists really don't like the use of PUNISHMENT because it tells the person what SHOULD NOT be done but not what SHOULD be done. Further, they note that punishment causes resentment, reduces communication, and leads to behavior that avoids the cause of the

## FIGURE 3-6
### BEHAVIORAL APPROACH

punishment. Under such conditions, people are likely to work just hard enough to "get by"—just enough to avoid punishment.

Behaviorists prefer the technique of EXTINCTION to punishment when undesirable behavior is observed. Extinction involves the absence of reward or positive reinforcement—essentially ignoring the undesired behavior. According to the behaviorists, people who are conditioned to expect positive reinforcement (reward) should detect its absence and eventually change their behavior to regain approval—more positive reinforcement.

Finally, there is a technique known as NEGATIVE REINFORCE-MENT. This involves the removal of an undesirable factor or activity—for instance, an unpopular work rule—if subordinates are "good".[8]

**COMMENT:**
The primary theme of the behaviorists is showing people the right way and giving them lots of "strokes" when they're doing the right thing. Behaviorists tend to object to the negative orientations of "traditional" dealings with people—"THOU SHALT NOT do this or that".

Let's take, for example, the case of the Budini Beer Company, a relatively obscure brewery somewhere in the wilds of New Jersey. Budini Beer, a derivative of an old Sicilian formula, is pretty bad stuff. However, it is popular with the motorcycle set and is known as "the brew for brutes and their broads". Many of the workers in the brewery chew tobacco. Management, concerned that careless spitting might degrade the sensitive bouquet of the beer, is tempted to place "DON'T SPIT" (thou shalt not) signs all over the brewery. However, after consultation with behaviorists, instead the brewery has many "SPIT HERE" (desired behavior) signs strategically located.

Obviously, the behaviorists stress REWARD POWER and use COER-CIVE POWER very sparingly if at all (unless that pat on the back is essential to your health). This approach seems quite manipulative—and it is. Behavior is being modified to suit the will of the person with the power to reward.

How frequently does the leader reward? Research has indicated that CONTINUOUS REINFORCEMENT (praise immediately after *each* desired behavior) is particularly effective when the subordinate is learning initially. PARTIAL REINFORCEMENT (intermittent rewards for *exceptional* performance only) is better when attempting to change behavior permanently.[9]

While the behaviorists get "credited" with many of the problems associated with modern-day permissiveness, their findings do help us understand how people tick.

# FEAR AS A MOTIVATOR

Our review of theories views Man as aggressively "reaching out"—sparking to achieve some desired goal. It should be recognized that much human behavior is associated with avoidance of some consequences based on fear. Many people focus their sparks more AWAY from things than TOWARD goals. This behavior could be associated with Maslow's SECURITY NEED. It has been said that the world is full of "success seekers" and "failure avoiders". Things aren't all that simple, but many people develop basic orientations due to personal experiences. Many who observed the misery of the Great Depression are likely to be extremely cautious about money matters. The nuclear balance of power concept relies on fear as a powerful motivator—the major power *must* fear the consequences of initiating a nuclear holocaust. Some bosses use fear as a tool for getting subordinates to do their bidding. We will discuss the effectiveness of this approach later on.

# LOVE AND HATE AS MOTIVATORS

There is ample evidence that both love and hate can be extraordinarily intense emotions contributing to huge sparks within people. Some leaders have been able to manipulate love of someone or something (one's country, for example) into intense hate for someone or something else (the enemy, for example). Many military leaders feel that fighting men must be conditioned to hate the enemy if they are to be effective in the gruesome business of war. We won't go further into this complicated subject. Just remember that both love and hate can be powerful motivators. Further, motivation based on love or hate can go to extremes—behavior that just doesn't make sense to those who don't share those emotions.

## COMMENT:

That just about wraps up the theoretical stuff. Remember that you've just taken the "crash course"—there's a lot more we just didn't have time for.

# PRACTICAL APPLICATIONS OF THEORIES

Some of these theoretical approaches probably cause frustrations for those who serve "in the trenches" in challenging leadership positions. Most appear to be based on optimistic views of people; many smack of the controlled conditions of the laboratory rather than the harsh realities of getting a tough job done. How much actual leading and managing have these researchers done? Let's attempt to put some of these theories to use by asking and responding to some practical questions.

*What happens when people spark to achieve a goal and progress toward that goal is either blocked or delayed?*

These people get frustrated. Their reactions vary. One might react violently and become aggressive. Another might shrug his shoulders and say, "the hell with it". Still another might become regressive (return to an immature mode of behavior) and scream, "If I can't have my way, I'll hold my breath 'til I turn blue!" Some people can adapt to frustration well; for others stress, anxiety and actual illness may result. Leaders must be able to deal with their own anxiety, stress and frustration. Further, they should be able to empathize with subordinates, to anticipate when they will encounter frustration and, when appropriate, to help them over the "rough spots".

*You talk about making jobs more challenging and interesting. What about those jobs that are, by their very nature, dull, monotonous and boring?*

Whenever possible and practical, GIVE THOSE JOBS TO MACHINES. They don't get bored. However, often this isn't possible. If the job is important, let people know and give the job more status. Consider giving the people more freedom if they can handle it. However, all of your efforts in this area may be to no avail. You may have to throw up your hands and just assume that employees doing that particular job will not be "motivated". Meanwhile, do the best you can. Treat them as adults (Argyris), provide enough extrinsic rewards to avoid dissatisfaction (Herzberg) and try to select people whose needs for achievement aren't particularly high (McClellan). Maybe you can satisfy some of their social needs (Maslow) by allowing them to work with those they like. In the meantime, recognize that they deserve your loyalty and that they can often be the source of productive ideas.

**COMMENT:**

Remember that the definition of "dull and monotonous" jobs can vary among individuals. Take the case of Flatus Flatlux, a successful professional who lived in an affluent suburban area. Whereas his home was lovely, his yard was a disaster. His beady-eyed neighbor with the green thumb, Hector Humus, took great delight in pointing out the demarcation between yards—a deep green carpet edged next to a scene of environmental pollution.

Finally, Flatus could take it no longer. He arranged for several chemical sprays and set aside a day to thatch, rake and seed his yard—in essence, to "build" a new yard. He was up at the crack of dawn renting equipment and setting up the task despite threatening weather. His teen-age son screamed with pain as he was dragooned into hours of heavy labor. In fact, his son dragged his feet all day long, taking advantage of several escape opportunities. Undaunted, Flatus toiled throughout the day in a

WHAT TURNS PEOPLE ON AND OFF?

cold drizzle until the job was done. His motivation was overwhelming; he was actually enjoying the experience.

WHY? What accounted for Flatus' huge sparks while his wretched son had none? Did Flatus embody the "work ethic" while his son was a "typical" malingering product of an affluent society? Obviously, this explanation is a bit simplistic and unfair.

The "dumb job" had special meaning to Flatus—a yard that would turn his arrogant neighbor green with envy. Further, Flatus needed the exercise. Physical work was a welcome change in his normal routine. For his son, who couldn't care less about the neighbor or the lawn, it was another job (he cut lawns in the neighborhood for spending money) supervised by some deranged "madman". Further, the son could probably visualize the extra work associated with mowing the revitalized lawn next summer. In essence, the task symbolized very different things to the two individuals. Effective leaders develop a "feel" for how their subordinates view their work.

*What about people who either can't or won't "generate sparks" in the workplace?*

This is a tough question for the leader because it indicates that he/she has, by definition, been unsuccessful, BUT YOU CAN'T WIN THEM ALL.

Let's face it. Some people have been conditioned throughout their formative years to believe that work is something to be avoided. They conform almost exactly to McGregor's Theory X view of Man. Other people may have been motivated at one time but have decided to "bank their sparks" at work and to "retire in place" somewhat prematurely. Still others may be unable to generate sparks due to problems with health, drugs or alcohol. Some may be suffering from "burnout"; they feel betrayed by a system which hasn't provided the expected rewards.

The leader is faced with three alternatives: (a) tolerate the absence of motivation, (b) remove the unmotivated worker from the workplace, or (c) keep trying to improve the situation.

Toleration avoids confrontation, but it also involves costs. Absence of motivation can be infectious, particularly if the unmotivated worker becomes a role model for others or creates unfair conditions for fellow workers. A transfer to another location in the organization shifts the problem elsewhere, but it does give the problem worker another chance under different conditions. Often the "chemistry" between a boss and a particular subordinate contributes to explosions rather than harmony—a change to another boss just may be the "solution". Sometimes, leaders do unmotivated workers a genuine favor by firing them—some people need a real shock to realize that a change in behavior is in order. Of course, firing, the "ultimate punishment" in the modern workplace, should occur only after adequate warning (there are some exceptions for particularly severe offenses).

Whatever the decision, the unmotivated worker must NOT appear to share the same rewards as his/her more productive peers. If it appears that there is some hope for the subordinate, the leader could consider (a) determining where the person stands with regard to satisfied needs and appealing to higher-level needs (Maslow), (b) enriching the person's job and seeing how he/she responds (Herzberg), or (c) identifying desired behavior and continuously rewarding favorable response or ignoring undesired behavior (Skinner).

If all else fails, either let him go or place him where he will do the least damage. BY ALL MEANS don't place him in a leadership position where subordinates will be affected. If necessary, create a STAFF (non-supervisory) position well off the beaten path.

## COMMENT:

Isn't this terribly wasteful? It certainly is, but many organizations have built-in security features that make it necessary.

### Is money a motivator or not?

Literally thousands of pages have been written on this subject; this response will be brief. It has been noted that "the nice thing about money is that it has such a wide circle of admirers." For sure, adequate wages and salaries contribute to employee decisions to join organizations. The question is whether people will work HARDER for MORE money.

According to the ECONOMIC MAN approach to motivation, money is THE PRIMARY MOTIVATOR. Those people living at the bottom two levels of Maslow's hierarchy naturally value money highly. Money doesn't lose all flavor at the upper levels. Very often, a person's self-esteem is related directly to what money brings; the trappings of wealth are strong motivators. For some, self-actualization may involve the goal of a million dollar annual income. Many compensation systems, particularly those associated with sales, tie income directly to productivity (commissions). However, it should be recognized that, for many people, other non-monetary factors become important when the person is making "enough".

Since people are different, it might be acceptable to allow them to "vote" concerning the incentives offered them. One approach to this idea is the "cafeteria system" of compensation where the employee can tailor the distribution of his/her total compensation according to individual needs and interests.

*My employees seem to be highly motivated to "rip me off". How can I discourage various forms of employee theft, white collar crime and abuse of rules?*

Quick and severe punishment of those who are caught is one approach. However, such controls, if abused, are likely to make the leader and the organization "the enemy". A cold, impersonal organizational environment with the employer demonstrating little or no loyalty to employees can have the same result.

It would be ideal if the organization could get its employees to feel like members of a team—"when you steal from the team, you steal from all of us". This is almost impossible for short-term, part-time employees. For them, just keep the temptations at a minimum. However, for others, it should be possible to appeal to their sense of loyalty remembering that "loyalty does not bubble up from the bottom; it trickles down from the top" (Small Paul to the Benedict Arnold Society, 71:41).

Remember that many employees view the organization as a large establishment with virtually limitless resources—"Who's going to miss a dollar or two? I really need the money". Some firms eliminate wages (pay by the hour) and put everyone on salary (evidence of trust) or go all the way on the team idea and share ownership with employees. The goal is to develop in them a proprietary interest in the long-term health and welfare of the concern. People are unlikely to rip themselves off.

*Just what is job enrichment all about?*

Job enrichment, or vertical job loading, is commonly associated with Frederick Herzberg and involves a focus on Herzberg's MOTIVATORS— achievement, recognition, responsibility, advancement, personal growth and the work itself.

How do you do it? Consider the following.

● Remove some controls over subordinates; show more confidence in their work.

● Make subordinates more accountable for their own work.

● Give subordinates complete tasks rather than parts of a task with others involved; let them relate to a "complete product".

● Give subordinates more authority and freedom.

● Introduce subordinates to more challenging tasks; allow them to become "experts".

● Give subordinates more feedback concerning their work; give them more personal recognition[10]

**COMMENT:**
Let's take the case of your secretary, Juliette Joy, the sweet young woman with the industrial-strength perfume and the office record for total time in

the ladies' room. Juliette typically types letters that you dictate or prepare in pencil. In turn, you proof them. If they're OK, you sign them; Juliette folds them, shoves them into the envelope, licks the envelope and off they go. This process consumes lots of your time, and you're very busy.

One day, after reading about job enrichment, you turn to Juliette and ask, "Juliette, how would you like to get enriched?" Juliette recoils, crosses her legs and looks for her handbag where she keeps a can of Mace. After some explanation, Juliette relaxes, goes to the ladies' room for an hour and finally says she'll give it a try.

Initially, you discontinue proofing the letters she types. Juliette seems to appreciate this and appears to put more effort into her work. In fact, a week later she bursts into your office during a high-level meeting and pleads, *"Enrich me again!"*

You turn over to her the preparation of all routine correspondence. Now Juliette's really perking. Occasionally, she stays late to complete a job. She begs for more. Pretty soon, she's typing, proofing and actually signing many of the letters for you. You now have time to plan ahead and do other worthwhile things appropriate for a person of your stature. Job enrichment has worked!

Does this sound like risky business? Does it appear that Juliette is "eating the bottom" out of your job? For sure, she is. Be prepared for her to ask for more money after a while.

Leaders who have a Theory X view of people (McGregor) are unlikely to entrust subordinates with so much freedom and authority. Insecure leaders who aren't willing to be accountable for an occasional mistake (Juliette is likely to make more mistakes than you do) might consider this lunacy.

However, if you have sharp people and are genuinely committed to their growth AND development AND MOTIVATION, job enrichment might be worth a try. Remember that job enrichment means adding more RESPONSIBILITY to the job. Don't confuse it with JOB ENLARGEMENT (horizontal job loading), which adds VARIETY BUT NO ADDITIONAL RESPONSIBILITY to the job. Adding variety to a dumb job (more dumb jobs) may reduce monotony, but it won't necessarily contribute to enhanced motivation.

*Are there other techniques related to job enrichment that might contribute to enhanced employee motivation?*

Absolutely. Job enrichment is closely related to a wide variety of contemporary management initiatives that reflect increased confidence in and respect for subordinates. These approaches are associated with a PARTICIPATIVE style of leadership. They include such techniques as Management by Objectives (MBO), quality circles, quality of work life

## FIGURE 3-7
### "I'VE BEEN ENRICHED!"

(QWL) programs, flexitime, self-management and others. But, HARK, this chapter is long enough now. We'll address some of these later in the book.

## SUMMARY

This chapter selectively touched the high points of what we know about what turns people on and off. While no one theory explains fully why people behave as they do, each provides some hints that are useful. The leader should understand how and why people "spark"—generate energy in order to accomplish things they want. With this understanding, the leader should be able to develop an organizational environment that satisfies *most* of the needs of BOTH the organization AND its members.

## NOTES

[1]Morris Massey, *The People Puzzle: Understanding Yourself and Others* (Reston, VA: Reston Publishing Company, Inc., 1979), p. 214.

[2]Douglas McGregor, *The Human Side of Enterprise* (New York: McGraw-Hill, Inc., 1960).

[3]Chris Argyris, *Personality and Organization* (New York: Harper & Row, 1957).

[4]Abraham Maslow, *Motivation and Personality*, 2d ed. (New York: Harper & Row, 1970).

[5]David C. McClellan, "Power Is the Great Motivator", *Harvard Business Review*, March/April, 1976, pp. 100-110.

[6]Frederick Herzberg, "One More Time: How Do You Motivate Employees?", *Harvard Business Review*, January-February, 1968, pp. 53-62.

[7]Victor Vroom, *Work and Motivation* (New York: John Wiley & Sons., 1964); L.W. Porter and E.E. Lawler, *Managerial Attitudes and Performance* (Homewood, IL: Richard D. Irwin, 1968).

[8]B.F. Skinner, *Contingencies of Reinforcement* (New York: Appleton Crofts, 1969).

[9]Fred Luthans and Robert Kreitner, *Organizational Behavior Modification* (New York: Scott, Foresman, 1975), p. 51.

[10]Herzberg, "One More Time: How Do You Motivate Employees?", pp. 53-62.

# WHAT DOES THE RESEARCH TELL US ABOUT LEADERSHIP?

"There are at least three subjects . . . on which no wise man should ever attempt to write: love, genius and leadership. Of the three, the last is the most mysterious . . . ."

Henri Peyre [1]

**COMMENT:**
This could be a very lengthy and tedious chapter. Grit your teeth; it may be just that. However, I will attempt to spare you as best I can and highlight only those results of research that you should put into your "kit bag of potentially useful knowledge". Despite my efforts, you're going to encounter some frustrations. Much of the research and many of the theories derived therefrom are inconclusive—there are far too many "yes, buts" and "what ifs". In many cases, the authorities just plain disagree among one another. If this chapter is to be useful for you, I'm going to have to interject my personal judgments based on my own research and personal experiences.

## WHAT ARE LEADERS' LIVES LIKE?

Henry Mintzberg's book, *The Nature of Managerial Work*, provides a revealing view of what "typical" managers do and how their lives tend to be different from those of others. Mintzberg's focus is on managers; I claim that the observations apply to leaders also. Prior to Mintzberg's study, the manager's roles were viewed as an orderly combination of POSDCORB—Planning, Organizing, Staffing, Directing, Coordinating, Reporting and Budgeting. Mintzberg's research provided a somewhat different view of the manager (and, for that matter, the leader):

- "Typical" managers feel compelled to perform great quantities of work at an unrelenting pace with little "free" time.
- Managers' work lives are characterized by brevity, variety and fragmentation; interruptions are commonplace; many activities are completed in minutes or seconds.
- Managers are attracted to the action-oriented, non-routine aspects of their jobs; routine activities are often viewed as "burdens".
- Managers spend a great deal of time communicating with others. Most favor oral, face-to-face techniques.
- The manager's job reflects a blend of duties and rights that he/she cannot "escape" after work because of the continuous nature of his/her responsibilities.[2]

## COMMENT:

Many people in today's highly specialized society live routine, repetitive lives. This type of life appeals to many people; they value certainty and security. However, if you're going to be responsible for other people, expect a life where each day is a bit unique and unpredictable. Further, be prepared for some long hours; convincing people to modify their behavior can take time.

## WHAT DO LEADERS DO?

So far, our focus has been upon the interactions between the leader and his/her immediate subordinates. However, it must be remembered that leaders—at least effective leaders—also affect their peers, their superiors and THE EXTERNAL ENVIRONMENT—THEY MAKE THINGS HAPPEN THAT WOULD NOT OTHERWISE HAPPEN. Listed below is one view of what leaders do:

- The leader as an *executive* serves as a coordinator of group activities.
- The leader as a *planner* serves to influence the ways and means a group achieves its assigned goals.
- The leader as a *policy maker* serves as a work group representative to higher levels in establishing goals and policies.
- The leader as an *expert* serves as a source of information and skills.
- The leader as *external group representative* serves as a work group representative in dealing with other groups.
- The leader as a *purveyor of rewards and punishments* serves as a recognizer of excellence and a disciplinarian.
- The leader as *arbitrator and mediator* serves as judge and conciliator of conflict within the group.
- The leader as *exemplar* serves as a model for the behavior of other work group members.
- The leader as *symbol of the group* serves as a focus for group unity.

• The leader as *scapegoat* serves as a target of criticism when things go wrong.[3]

Thus, we see that GETTING PEOPLE TO DO THINGS—WILL-INGLY involves a variety of activities and perspectives. Just to add some "balance" to the list, above (reference to *scapegoat*), we should note that the leader can serve as the *hero or heroine* when things go right. Now that we know what leaders do, it would be nice to know HOW TO DO IT RIGHT.

## WHAT ARE *EFFECTIVE* LEADERS LIKE?

Early attempts to fathom the "mysteries" of leadership focused on the "traitest" approach—an attempt to identify those traits common to successful leaders. The idea was that, with such traits identified, pro-spective leaders could concentrate on acquiring them and, thus, be guaranteed leadership success. The idea was doomed from the start. A leader's success is measured by the performance of his/her subordinates. It was finally acknowledged that there are far too many variables, many of which the leader can't control, that influence that performance. Some truly magnificent people were labeled ineffective leaders as a result of bad luck. Adolph Hitler's success—and he certainly was successful for a while—remains a mystery to many.

**COMMENT:**
With such an indictment of the "traitest" approach, why go further? The bushels of research on this subject reveal some characteristics that are quite (not completely) consistent and, thus, deserve your attention. Take a look at some of the lists that follow. If you've got a bunch of these characteristics, grab a group of people, call them subordinates and see how you do.

Some of the early research focusing on traits of successful leaders found the "typical" leader to be a white male from a wealthy family who was TALLER, HEAVIER and HANDSOMER than average. All of these have since been rejected except socio-economic status. It seems that offspring of successful parents do have a better chance to be successful leaders than offspring of less successful parents.

**COMMENT:**
If you're tall, muscular and handsome, don't be offended. You've still got a chance, but you've got to fight it out with women, minorities and "Little People". However, remember we are in the age of miniaturization—"small is beautiful"—we're learning a lot about leadership from the Japanese; watch out for the munchkins.

Bernard Bass conducted a detailed analysis of the results of many surveys that attempted to identify the traits common to successful leaders. Bass concluded that, based on the survey data, the effective leader is most frequently characterized by:

- A strong drive for responsibility and task completion.
- Vigor and persistence in pursuit of goals.
- Venturesomeness and originality in problem solving.
- Drive to exercise initiative in social situations.
- Self-confidence and a sense of personal identity.
- Willingness to accept consequences of decisions and actions.
- Readiness to absorb interpersonal stress.
- Willingness to tolerate frustration and delay.
- Ability to influence other persons' behavior.
- Capacity to structure social interaction systems to the purpose at hand.[4]

David Brown conducted a survey of nearly 1000 supervisors and managers, asking them to identify those qualities they most preferred in their leaders. The following five consistently rated above others:

- Respect and feeling for others.
- Knowledge of the subject [the work of the group].
- Willingness to accept personal responsibility.
- Willingness to support "me" [the subordinate].
- A quality that indicates strength or confidence.[5]

Note that the preferences, above, were FROM THE PERSPECTIVE OF THE SUBORDINATE.

Not identified on the lists, above, but mentioned quite prominently in much literature are (a) integrity, (b) ability to communicate, (c) empathy (ability to identify with the emotions of others), (d) health and vigor and (e) basic intelligence.

**COMMENT:**
Wow! What a laundry list! Sounds like a leader has to be a combination of Joan of Arc and Superman in order to be effective. Not really, but it would help.

## WHAT ARE *INEFFECTIVE* LEADERS LIKE?

Returning to the survey by David Brown, 1107 persons were asked to identify the five characteristics that were most likely to cause them to "reject those in positions of leadership". Listed below are those characteristics that received the most frequent response:

- Inability to delegate; couldn't accept subordinate ideas.
- Dishonest or deceitful; lied to others.
- Did not support subordinates.

## FIGURE 4-1
## IDEAL LEADER CHARACTERISTICS
## MALE VERSION

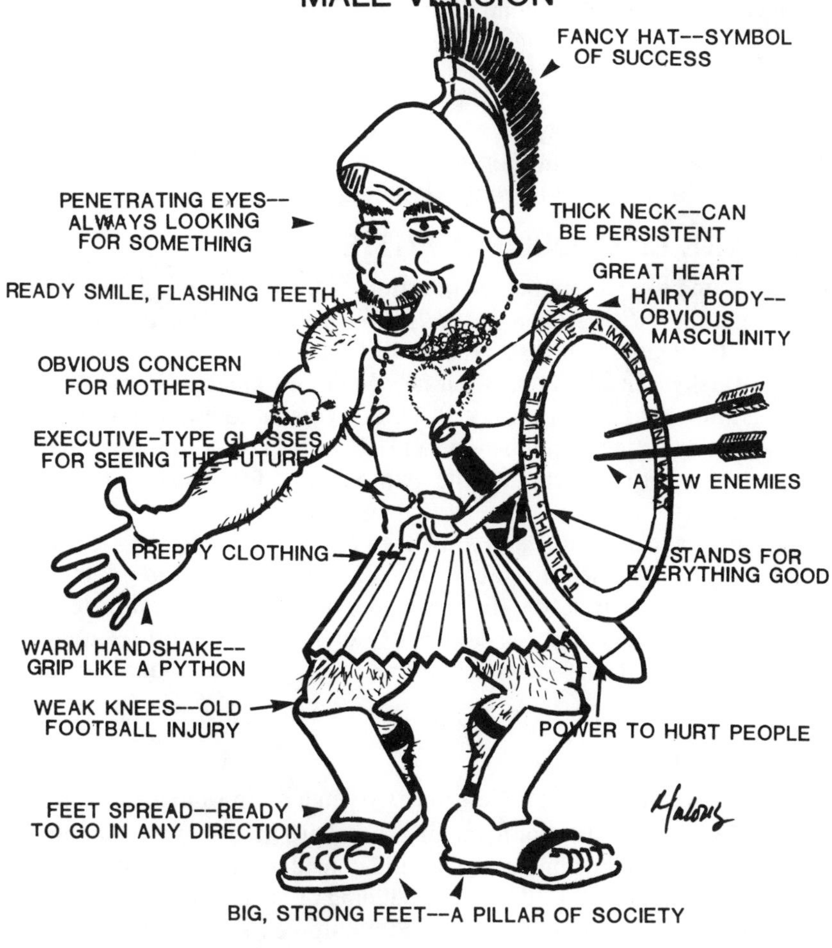

FANCY HAT--SYMBOL OF SUCCESS

PENETRATING EYES-- ALWAYS LOOKING FOR SOMETHING

THICK NECK--CAN BE PERSISTENT

READY SMILE, FLASHING TEETH

GREAT HEART
HAIRY BODY-- OBVIOUS MASCULINITY

OBVIOUS CONCERN FOR MOTHER

EXECUTIVE-TYPE GLASSES FOR SEEING THE FUTURE

A FEW ENEMIES

PREPPY CLOTHING

STANDS FOR EVERYTHING GOOD

WARM HANDSHAKE-- GRIP LIKE A PYTHON

WEAK KNEES--OLD FOOTBALL INJURY

POWER TO HURT PEOPLE

FEET SPREAD--READY TO GO IN ANY DIRECTION

BIG, STRONG FEET--A PILLAR OF SOCIETY

- Unable to make intelligent judgments or decisions.
- Reversed self often; indecisive.
- Completely inflexible.
- Lacked respect for or trust in others.
- Egotistical; interested only in self.
- Weak; no self-confidence.
- Inability to act; passive.
- Would not communicate with others.

- Unwilling or unable to give constructive help or guidance.
- Over-controlled others.
- Over-involved with details.
- Played favorites [favoritism to selected subordinates].[6]

**COMMENT:**
Note how character, integrity and honesty come up frequently. Fortunately, neither you nor I am guilty of any of the sins, above. However, many such people live and breathe in modern organizations AND ATTEMPT TO LEAD. It's a "crime", but very few go to jail for it.

## WHAT ARE LEADERS' PRIORITIES?

This may sound like a complicated question, but it really isn't. Leadership involves getting *PEOPLE* to do *THINGS*—willingly. The two BASIC aspects of the leadership task are the PEOPLE (subordinates) and the THINGS (tasks). Leaders are often faced with an inner conflict—"how much attention do I focus on my PEOPLE versus how much attention do I focus on getting the job done (THE TASK)?" Variations in the allocation of priorities between the two account for various styles of leadership.

Two major research efforts that focused on the BEHAVIOR OF THE LEADERS (as opposed to the characteristics of the leaders in the "traitest" approach that we discussed previously) were conducted at Ohio State University and the University of Michigan. Both examined the conflict between the leader's concern for subordinates and concern for the task.

### Ohio State Studies

The Ohio State studies identified the two leadership dimensions as (a) CONSIDERATION (development of mutual trust, two-way communication, respect for subordinates' ideas and consideration of their feelings) and (b) INITIATING STRUCTURE (defining or structuring group activities to get the job done). The Ohio State studies showed that BOTH consideration AND initiating structure are necessary for successful performance; an effective leader is BOTH demanding AND sensitive to the needs of subordinates; a leader should be flexible since the proper balance of priorities varies according to the situation.[7]

### University of Michigan Studies

The University of Michigan studies, under the direction of Rensis Likert, were designed to identify styles of leadership that resulted in both high levels of work group performance and high levels of satisfaction. Two distinct styles of leadership were examined:

**FIGURE 4-2**

**EXTREME APPROACHES TO LEADERSHIP**

JOB-CENTERED

EMPLOYEE-CENTERED

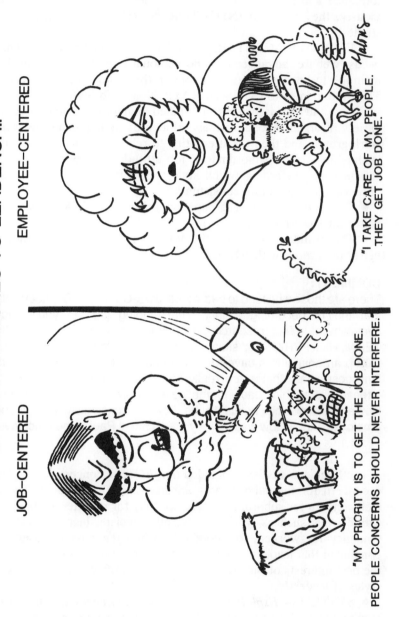

"MY PRIORITY IS TO GET THE JOB DONE. PEOPLE CONCERNS SHOULD NEVER INTERFERE."

"I TAKE CARE OF MY PEOPLE. THEY GET JOB DONE."

- JOB-CENTERED leaders are detatched and uninvolved with their subordinates. They exercise close supervision, pressure for better performance and focus on meeting deadlines and evaluating output. Obviously, they relate to INITIATING STRUCTURE in the Ohio State studies.

- EMPLOYEE-CENTERED leaders are concerned with employee needs, welfare, advancement and personal growth. They consider their main job to be supervision of people rather than expediting production. This style relates to CONSIDERATION at Ohio State.

Likert and his associates conducted hundreds of studies in a wide variety of organizational settings (a) identifying high- and low-producing work groups and then (b) attempting to relate the supervisors' styles of leadership to their subordinates' job attitudes and performance. While conclusions concerning which style was better were a bit vague, two observations were quite consistent:

- The performance of groups with JOB-CENTERED leaders was better for short-term, high-priority tasks.

- The attitudes of groups with EMPLOYEE-CENTERED leaders were better than those with JOB-CENTERED leaders.

**COMMENT:**
There are those who tend to bad-mouth JOB-CENTERED leaders, claiming that they're becoming extinct. That's going too far; you'll find them everywhere. In fact, research indicates that they do very well in SHORT-TERM, HIGH-PRIORITY situations. Remember the words of the Big Book, "Keep an animal in a cave for emergencies. Roll back the rock and turn him loose when things are really foul. Then, when he's got everyone's attention, drag him back to the cave before he gums everything up. However, allow his howls to be heard occasionally just to let your employees know how well off they are." (Small Paul to the Machiavellians, 17:51.)

The Michigan studies concluded that *BOTH* a concern for the task and a concern for the subordinates are necessary for success. Those who lack concern for subordinates tend to "pay for it" after a while, often in subtle ways such as work quality, absenteeism, high quit rates and a tendency for workers to "goof off" when the boss is absent. Likert concluded that leadership styles that maximize human satisfaction are in the best interests of the organization. He identified four basic systems or styles of leadership:

- SYSTEM I—*Exploitative Authoritative*: Leaders literally "use" and manipulate their subordinates focusing on the task, making all of the decisions and caring little for the welfare of subordinates.

# FIGURE 4-3

# "KEEP AN ANIMAL IN A CAVE"

"OH, HIM? THE COMPANY KEEPS
HIM AROUND FOR CRISIS SITUATIONS."

● SYSTEM II—*Benevolent Authoritative*: Leaders focus on the task and make all of the decisions but care for their subordinates much as a parent treats his/her children.

● SYSTEM III—*Consultative*: Leaders focus both on the task and the subordinates and consult with subordinates concerning decisions relating to the workplace.

● SYSTEM IV—*Participative*: Leaders focus both on the task and the subordinates and include subordinates in the planning and decision making processes.

**COMMENT:**
According to Likert, low-producing organizations tend to have Systems I and II leaders; high-producing firms, Systems III and IV. Likert inferred that System IV should be the "goal" of all organizations but recognized that most today are somewhere between System II and System III.[8]

### The Blake and Mouton Managerial Grid

Note that both the Ohio State and the Michigan studies conclude that considerable attention should be given by leaders to BOTH people and the task REGARDLESS OF SITUATION. The research of Robert R. Blake and Jane S. Mouton reaches the same conclusion. They are world famous for their Managerial Grid, which is shown in Figure 4-4. Note that the axes are the two factors we discussed previously—concern (by the leader) for production or task (horizontal), and concern for people (vertical). Blake and Mouton concluded that the relative degree of concern by the leader is the key variable relating to leadership effectiveness.

The grid allows us to "plot" leadership styles using its coordinates and then to compare such styles with an "ideal" style. Let's take a quick tour around the grid and examine some characteristics of leadership styles at various "critical points".

● AUTHORITY-OBEDIENCE LEADER (9,1—lower right-hand corner): Efficiency in operations results from arranging conditions of work in such a way that human elements interfere to a minimum degree.

● COUNTRY CLUB LEADER (1,9—upper left-hand corner): Thoughtful attention to needs of people for satisfying relationships leads to a comfortable, friendly organizational atmosphere and work tempo.

● IMPOVERISHED LEADER (1,1—lower left-hand corner):
Exertion of minimum effort to get required work done is appropriate to sustain organizational membership.

● ORGANIZATION MAN LEADER (5,5—middle of graph): Adequate organizational performance is possible through balancing the necessity to get out work with maintaining morale of people at a satisfactory level.

# FIGURE 4-4

# THE MANAGERIAL GRID

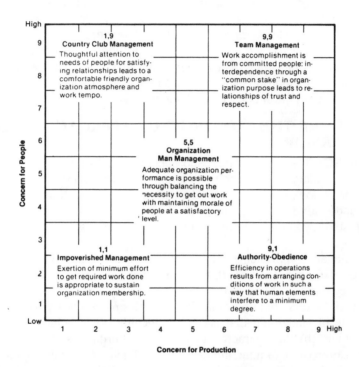

The Managerial Grid figure from *The New Managerial Grid*, by Robert R. Blake and Jane Srygley Mouton. Houston: Gulf Publishing Company, Copyright © 1978, page 11. Reproduced by permission.

● TEAM MANAGEMENT LEADER (9,9—upper right-hand corner): Work accomplishment is from committed people; interdependence through a "common stake" in organizational purpose leads to relationships of trust and respect.[9]

The Managerial Grid is used extensively in organizational development programs—programs designed to enhance organizational effectiveness through, in part, improved leadership. The objective is to move the organizational climate and the leaders toward a 9,9 TEAM MANAGE-MENT LEADER style, the style considered by Blake and Mouton to be "ideal" for all situations. Blake and Mouton have devised a six-phase program under which leaders (a) identify their current style (on the grid) and then (b) work toward a 9,9 approach.

**COMMENT:**
Note that all of the BEHAVIORAL approaches to leadership (focusing on leader styles and behavior) appear to agree—the 9,9 leader is a "winner" and, thus, the way to go for MOST situations; total commitment to BOTH the task AND the subordinates is an "ideal" leadership style.

It would be nice if we could stop here, but there are those who insist on "muddying the water". They claim that it isn't all that simple; there isn't an "ideal" style appropriate for all situations. They advocate a "situational" or "contingency" approach to leadership.

## WHAT ARE THE CONTINGENCY APPROACHES TO LEADERSHIP?

WARNING: The contingency approaches that follow make for some "heavy" reading. If you're going to grasp their messages, you should take the time to look carefully at the figures and diagrams that are provided and understand their significance. If you're a bit fatigued right now, I suggest that you defer further reading until you're fresh.

Contingency approaches are essentially "if-then" approaches—IF certain conditions prevail, THEN a particular technique of leadership is preferred. The problem is that the theorists disagree about which conditions or factors are important. The variables most often associated with the style of leadership that is "best" include (a) the characteristics of the leader, (b) the characteristics of the subordinates, (c) the type of organization (for example, military and academic organizations have very different characteristics) and (d) the nature of the environment within which the organization operates (for example, crisis situations versus routine operations).

### Douglas McGregor

You'll recall our previous discussion of Douglas McGregor and his Theories X and Y. Leaders cannot engage in "unnatural acts" in the workplace. A leader who, deep down in his/her heart, does not believe that subordinates can operate with freedom, is unlikely to allow any degree of participative management within his/her organization. Conversely, a leader who has had more favorable experiences with people and is, thus, more optimistic about them, can be "comfortable" with sharing decision making with subordinates. Note how perspectives of people in general in Figure 4-5 influence leadership styles and even political systems.

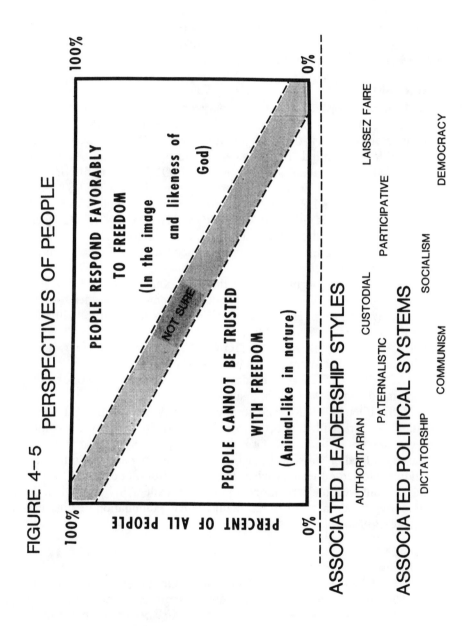

FIGURE 4–5    PERSPECTIVES OF PEOPLE

**COMMENT:**
Draw an imaginary vertical line somewhere along Figure 4-5; your views are portrayed somewhere along the continuum. Some (a certain percentage) people can be trusted with freedom; others cannot. The leadership style that is "best" for you will be influenced by your view of how much freedom your subordinates can "tolerate".

### Fred Fiedler

Fred Fiedler's approach relates to McGregor's X and Y views of people. According to Fiedler, an individual's leadership style is a function of his/her personality and is, thus, pretty well fixed by the time he/she is an adult. With this in mind, Fiedler says (a) find out what kind of a person you are and then (b) adapt the WORK ENVIRONMENT to fit your (the leader's) personality. Fiedler designed a test involving a LEAST PRE-FERRED COWORKER index. According to Fiedler, the test will reveal whether the person is either (a) RELATIONSHIP-ORIENTED (concern for people, consideration, etc.) or (b) TASK-ORIENTED (concern for task, initiating structure, etc.). Note that, according to Fiedler, you are one extreme or the other.

The other dimension in Fiedler's theory is known as "SITUATION FAVORABLENESS"—the degree a situation enables a leader to exert influence over a group. He identified three factors to measure "situation favorableness" (see Figure 4-6):

 • LEADER-MEMBER RELATIONS—The degree of respect, admiration and trust that subordinates have for the leader.

 • TASK STRUCTURE—The degree to which a group's work can be programmed and spelled out in a step-by-step fashion.

 • POSITION POWER—The formal authority vested in the leader's position (leaders with authority to reward and fire have high position power).

Based on Fiedler's research, task-oriented leaders perform better than relationship-oriented leaders when the three factors, above, are "favorable" or "unfavorable"; relationship-oriented leaders do better when the factors are "moderate" or in the middle.[10] An examination of Figure 4-7 is necessary to follow this process.

**COMMENT:**
Just follow these steps:
 • STEP ONE—Find out which style of leader you are, using Fiedler's Least Preferred Coworker test and index or some other technique.
 • STEP TWO—Plot the characteristics of your work environment, using the three factors in Figure 4-7 (this will locate your "situation" in one of the eight combinations in Figure 4-7).

## FIGURE 4-6
## FIEDLER'S THEORY

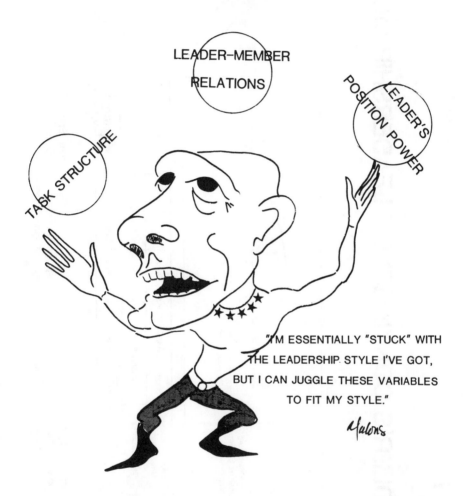

"I'M ESSENTIALLY "STUCK" WITH THE LEADERSHIP STYLE I'VE GOT, BUT I CAN JUGGLE THESE VARIABLES TO FIT MY STYLE."

● STEP THREE—If your style "fits" (you have the style which, according to Fiedler, is correct for the situation), do nothing—you're in "hog heaven", you're a winner. However, if you don't have the right style for the work situation, consider *changing one or more of the factors* until you have a "fit" (don't consider changing your personality since, according to Fiedler, you can't).

Let's consider the case of Yetta Yamaguchi, a 67-year-old woman of Polish extraction and supervisor of 20 production line employees at Kitty

# FIGURE 4-7

## FIEDLER'S CONTINGENCY LEADERSHIP MODEL

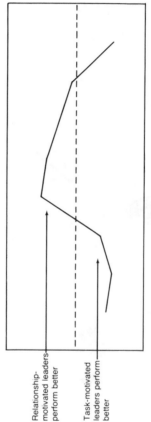

Reprinted by permission of the *Harvard Business Review*. An exhibit from "Engineer the Job to Fit the Manager" by Fred E. Fiedler (September/October 1965). Copyright © 1965 by the President and Fellows of Harvard College; all rights reserved.

Krunchies, Inc. According to Fiedler's Least Preferred Coworker scale, Yetta is a task-oriented leader (Step One). Yetta's relations with her subordinates are relatively poor; the production line work is highly repetitive (structured); Yetta has been delegated complete freedom to hire and fire subordinates (strong position power). Note that the work environment is located at position 5 in Figure 4-7 (Step Two). According to Fiedler's research, relationship-oriented leaders do better than task-oriented leaders "in the middle". What can Yetta do to improve her effectiveness? Fiedler says she can't change her style BUT perhaps she can change the work environment. If she improved her leader-member relations and, thus, moved to position 1 in Figure 4-7, there would, according to Fiedler, be a "fit" (Step Three).

Is Fiedler correct? He thinks he is, and he's in every textbook on the subject I've read.

**Vroom and Yetton**

Victor Vroom and Phillip Yetton are known for their Normative Theory of Leadership, which attempts to focus on HOW LEADERS SHOULD MAKE DECISIONS in a variety of situations. Vroom and Yetton first identified five decision making styles ranging from authoritative to participative and then came up with a series of seven questions that should be asked in order to determine the preferable style for the particular situation.

The seven questions center around whether (a) a high-quality decision is required, (b) the leader has all of the information to make the decision him/herself, and (c) subordinate acceptance of the decision is important. According to this approach, the leader should make the decision him/herself when the decision is relatively simple, the leader has all of the necessary information and the subordinates are relatively indifferent to the outcome. However, as decisions become more complex and require more information and as subordinates become more concerned, greater degrees of participation should be introduced.[11]

**COMMENT:**
Take the case of Boris Boronic, Commissar for Toilet Tissue for the Soviet Union. While not a prominent figure during May Day ceremonies, Boris is reasonably influential in that his product touches most of the Russian people. In fact Boris recently was awarded a Hero of Hygiene Medal, Second Class, for his development of a toilet paper roll with 10,000 sheets. Boris proved that savings associated with the roll would allow for production of two extra Mig-25 Foxbat interceptor aircraft per year. However, acceptance of the new roll has been poor. The roll is so large

that there's no place for the user to sit down in the rest room stall. The Soviet people complained claiming that this was too severe a sacrifice for extra interceptor aircraft.

Annually, Boris must make decisions concerning the design, manufacture, distribution and sale of toilet tissue for the Soviet Union. If the alternatives are limited, if no one really cares, Vroom and Yetton would recommend that Boris make the decision himself (Authoritative)—why bother making waves when a "high quality" decision isn't necessary? However, if the Russian people are aware of the advantages of "squeezably soft" toilet tissue, if they've seen that American commercial where a grandmother actually brings a roll of paper to her family on a commercial airliner, they'll realize how much they're missing. Further, if Boris' subordinates are likely to become emotionally involved in the decision and their support of the decision is essential to carrying it out, then Boris should consider Consultative or even Participative techniques.

### Blanchard and Hersey

Our final review of a contingency theory is based on research by Kenneth Blanchard and Paul Hersey. Blanchard and Hersey consider the "MATURITY OF SUBORDINATES" to be the critical variable that should determine which style of leadership is most effective for a particular situation. They define "maturity", not as age or emotional stability, but as desire for achievement, willingness to accept responsibility and task-related ability and experience. They believe that the relationship between the leader and the subordinates should, when appropriate, move through four phases as subordinates develop and "mature" and that leaders should vary their style with each phase. Unlike Fiedler, Hersey and Blanchard believe that it IS possible for the leader to modify his/her style.

Figure 4-8 portrays the "proper" trace of evolution of style according to Blanchard and Hersey. Note that it is very similar to the Blake and Mouton Managerial Grid with task behavior on the horizontal axis and relationships (people) behavior on the vertical axis. The added dimension, maturity of subordinates, is at the bottom of the figure moving from immature at the right to increasing maturity as one moves to the left. The curving line is the "way to go". For example, a high task, low relationships style (plotted as 9,1 on the managerial grid we discussed previously) is appropriate for particularly immature subordinates. As maturity increases, the "proper" style involves less focus on task and more focus on relationships UNTIL the mid-point. At that point, Blanchard and Hersey suggest a reduction of attention to both task and relationships.[12]

# FIGURE 4-8
# SITUATIONAL LEADERSHIP

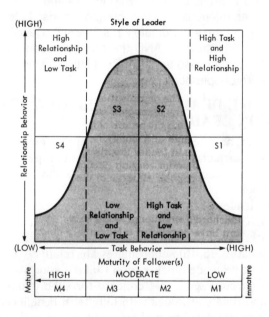

Paul Hersey/Kenneth H. Blanchard, *Management of Organizational Behavior: Utilizing Human Resources*, 4th ed., © 1982, p. 152. Reprinted by permission of Prentice-Hall, Inc., Englewood Cliffs, N.J.

**COMMENT:**

Take the unusual case of Wanda Wonderbar and her phenomenal success in Ignominious Industries. In a brief period of seven years, Wanda has been promoted from the lower levels of the Shipping Department to Executive Vice President. People credit her unique leadership skills for her achievement. How would Blanchard and Hersey account for this?

According to the Blanchard and Hersey approach, Wanda WAS able to adapt her leadership style to fit the maturity of her subordinates. First, when in the Shipping Department (presumably dealing with relatively "immature" subordinates), she was very task-oriented with little regard for relationships. As she climbed the rungs of the hierarchy and, thus, encountered increasingly mature subordinates, she reduced her focus on the task (mature subordinates know what to do without a lot of guidance) and increased her interests in their human needs. Later on, as she encountered very mature subordinates at the very top levels, she reduced her interests in BOTH the task AND the relationships (not only do they know what to do but they also tend to resent intrusions into their personal lives—truly mature people don't need it).

## WHAT CAN WE DERIVE FROM ALL OF THESE THEORIES ON LEADERSHIP?

First, it's clear that, despite lots of research, there's plenty of disagreement concerning what particular style of leadership fits a particular situation. That leaves the final decision up to you. That's the reason for Parts B and C of this book.

All agree that leadership style results from a blend of CONCERN FOR TASK and CONCERN FOR SUBORDINATES. Most would agree that concern for task is particularly important when (a) subordinates don't know exactly what to do, (b) subordinates are relatively unmotivated or (c) decisions must be made quickly (don't take a vote when the building is on fire). Most would agree that concern for subordinates contributes to favorable subordinate attitudes with long-term benefits *to include the development of future decision makers and leaders*.

Most agree that leadership styles designed for B-Bs are not likely to work well for GOLF BALLS, TENNIS BALLS or anything bigger. Many modern organizations were designed with a "B-B mentality". They are not likely to attract and retain the best people in the workforce. However, if you like B-Bs, they're out there—they just don't work very hard. It's a good idea to know what you're dealing with.

There is some disagreement concerning whether leadership can be learned and how much one individual can vary his/her style of leadership. Fiedler says you're essentially "stuck" with the style you've got and the utility of leadership training is questionable. Most of the other authorities disagree with Fiedler; I think they're right. An understanding of human behavior and all of its dimensions helps; leadership skills are enhanced with practice. Further, effective leaders are "flexible"; they can modify their styles within certain limits to fit particular situations.

## IF WE HAVE ALL OF THESE THEORIES AVAILABLE, WHY ARE THERE SO MANY INEFFECTIVE LEADERS AROUND?

This chapter illustrates one of the reasons. Leadership is tough to teach because the body of available knowledge is inconsistent and incomplete. Every practitioner must, to a degree, be his/her own "pioneer" exploring unknowns for him/herself.

Some leaders have never actually served as subordinates; they enter the workplace at a distinct disadvantage. I agree with Robert Townsend who says, "I don't think you can be a stand-out officer without having been a trooper. You have to know how workers think and talk."[13] General Melvin Zais expresses this point even more eloquently:

You need to be amused at their humor, you need to be tolerant of their bawdiness, and you have to understand that they're as lousy as you let them be, as good as you make them be. You just have to really like them and feel good about being with them.[14]

Far too often, people who do well at work are rewarded by a promotion to a leadership position. Whereas they can do the WORK very well, they don't know a thing about dealing with people; the reward for good performance forces them into positions where they perform poorly.

Leaders are frequently under considerable pressure to satisfy a wide variety of interest groups. Many ambitious people, in the process of climbing to positions of leadership, wind up becoming obligated to bosses or to the organization. When they have "invested" tremendous time and effort in achieving success by pleasing their bosses, some feel that they must sacrifice the needs of their subordinates in order to insure continued success.

**COMMENT:**

Take the case of Billy-Bob Budd, an idealistic and dynamic young man from Gumm County somewhere deep in the South. Billy-Bob had considerable charisma and a strong inner need to serve his fellow man. He ran for public office and won. He was considered an "ideal" public servant—dedicated, honest and totally committed to the needs of his constituents.

After Billy-Bob served several terms in office, he was faced with a particularly challenging election. Sensing a need for help in winning, he accepted the assistance of several strong interest groups. Of course, there were "strings" associated with that assistance. Billy-Bob was obliged to reimburse his benefactors in a variety of ways. Some of these "payments" were not in the public interest, but they were essential to his continued success. They made Billy-Bob feel uncomfortable, but he justified them in his mind by convincing himself that he was what Gumm County really needed. After a while, they seemed insignificant. To a degree, he had become a "hostage" of the system; he was no longer quite the same leader Gumm County once had.

Sometimes the power that goes with leadership positions has a corrupting influence on people; leaders lose contact with their subordinates; they become so preoccupied with "great things" that they forget how "ordinary people" feel.

**COMMENT:**
Take the case of Sam Septic, the developer of the Septic Sound Simulator. Sam was an exceptionally congenial and approachable man with a very creative mind. His ideas caught on and, in no time, Septic Simulations, Inc. grew from a garage laboratory operation to a multi-million dollar corporation.

As the organization grew, Sam's relationships with his subordinates changed. Sam became insulated from his old friends as he moved into a huge, mahogany-paneled office with two-inch rugs and a private john with a padded toilet seat. His schedule was rigidly controlled by a bevy of administrative assistants, aides and secretaries who made sure he was protected from the "trivia" asociated with "ordinary people". As time went by, he lost touch with those who had once contributed to his creativity; he became a very different kind of leader.

## SUMMARY

This chapter has involved a selective examination of the results of available research on the subject of leadership. While inconsistencies were recognized, each perspective provides an approach that can be considered when attempting the challenging task of GETTING PEOPLE TO DO THINGS—WILLINGLY. Recognizing that leadership is a highly personal process, it is now time to turn from theories and laboratory experiments to a specific personal approach. Part B, which follows, will do this.

## NOTES

[1]Henri Peyre, "Excellence and Leadership: Has Western Europe Any Lessons for Us?" in Stephen R. Graubard and Gerald Holton (eds.), *Excellence and Leadership in a Democracy* (New York: Columbia University Press, 1962), p. 1.

[2]Henry Mintzberg, *The Nature of Managerial Work* (New York: Harper & Row, 1973), pp. 51-53.

[3]David Krech, Richard S. Crutchfield and Egerton L. Ballachey, *Individual in Society: A Textbook in Social Psychology* (New York: McGraw Hill, 1962), pp. 428-430.

[4]Bernard M. Bass, *Stogdill's Handbook of Leadership* (New York: The Free Press, 1981), p. 81.

[5]David S. Brown, *Managing the Large Organization: Issues, Ideas, Precepts, Innovations* (Mt. Airy, MD: Lomond Books, 1982), p. 230.

[6]*Ibid.*, p. 232.

[7]Chester A. Schriesheim and Barbara J. Bird, "Contributions of the Ohio State Studies to the Field of Leadership", *Journal of Management*, Fall, 1974, pp. 135-145.

[8]Rensis Likert, *New Patterns of Management* (New York: McGraw-Hill, 1961); Rensis Likert, *The Human Organization* (New York: McGraw-Hill, 1967).

[9]Robert R. Blake and Jane S. Mouton, *The New Managerial Grid* (Houston: Gulf Publishing Company, 1978), p. 11.

[10]Fred E. Fiedler, "The Leadership Game: Matching the Man to the Situation", *Organizational Dynamics*, Winter, 1976, p. 11.

[11]Victor H. Vroom, "Can Leaders Learn to Lead?", *Organizational Dynamics*, Winter, 1976, pp. 17-28.

[12]Paul Hersey and Kenneth H. Blanchard, *Management of Organizational Behavior*, 3d Ed. (Englewood Cliffs, NJ: Prentice-Hall, Inc., 1979).

[13]Robert Townsend, *Further Up the Organization* (New York: Alfred A. Knopf, 1984), p. 11.

[14]Tom Peters and Nancy Austin, *A Passion for Excellence* (New York: Random House, 1985), p. 291.

# PART B

# BACK TO BERT AND BERTHA

NOTICE THAT THEY ARE NOW BIGGER BALLS.
THAT'S BECAUSE THEY READ PART A.

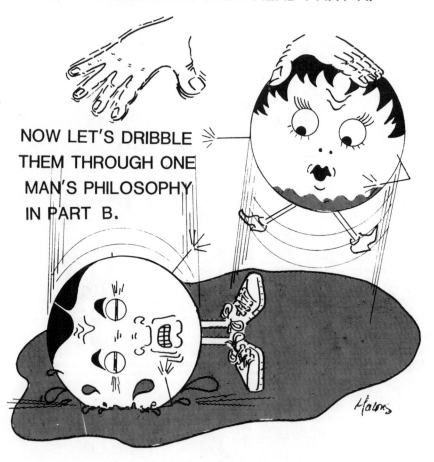

NOW LET'S DRIBBLE
THEM THROUGH ONE
MAN'S PHILOSOPHY
IN PART B.

# ONE MAN'S PHILOSOPHY OF LEADERSHIP

## OBJECTIVES OF PART B

With Part A sizzling in your mind, you are now "armed" with a profusion of terms, concepts and theories. Unfortunately, they don't "mesh" well; they produce discord rather than a symphony of coordinated thought. The fact is that there are too many unknowns; some theories disagree with one another; there is no "school solution". Meanwhile, you're interested in enhancing your own leadership effectiveness. How can YOU best prepare to GET PEOPLE TO DO THINGS—WILLINGLY? What approach works for YOU?

If I had a concise answer to that question, people would be beating a path to my door; I would be rich and famous rather than pounding on a personal computer in the depths of my basement. Instead, I plan to give you something to think about—MY philosophy of leadership. Each chapter that follows discusses one of MY COMMANDMENTS that you read in the Introduction. They've worked pretty well for me during my 33 years of professional life. However, they certainly don't apply to all situations, all organizations and all people. As you read them, be critical, look for flaws, SHOOT THEM TO PIECES! Remember that MY philosophy is of little consequence. If YOUR experience reading this book is to be of any value, it is that YOU develop YOUR OWN philosophy of leadership. Part C, which follows, is designed to help you do this.

## COMMENT:

Back to Bert and Bertha. Our "Dynamic Duo" are now going to be "dribbled" through one man's philosophy. Dribbling is excellent exercise; it stimulates the vital body juices and contributes to growth. In the process, Bert and Bertha are going to be splashed with many of my personal biases. That's OK; my commandments are "washable".

## POSSIBLE REACTIONS

Some who read my philosophy are likely to react violently. "My God, this clown is utterly naive and unrealistic. People would rip such a leader to shreds. He must be from the Land of Oz".

I'll acknowledge that I'm somewhat of an idealist and an optimist. I am influenced by the famous quote from the Big Book, "If you wake up in the morning and there's horse manure under your pillow, be sure that someone has given you a pony" (Small Paul to the Pessimissians, 39:11). I've been conditioned by generally rewarding experiences with people. During my 30 years in the Army, I met some M.A.S.H. stereotypes (uncommitted, bureaucratic bunglers) and some genuine foul balls for sure, but most of the people were decent and dedicated professionals. Even foul balls serve a useful purpose—BAD EXAMPLES. My subsequent experiences in business and academia have reinforced my impression that MOST people are "good".

I realize that the newspapers are full of evidence that leads to questions concerning my view of people. If you add up the number of child molesters, drug traffickers, tax evaders, insurance swindlers, exam cheaters, and porno peddlers, etc., in this country, the total would make one wince. Despite this, I hold that most people are "good"—bad news gets lots of attention and, I suspect, some double-counting.

## SOME COMPARISONS

If you're looking for a real contrast in philosophy, I suggest that you read *The Prince* by Niccolo Machiavelli. Machiavelli didn't mind a bit of deceit and treachery. People should, according to Machiavelli, be led through a process of crafty manipulation.[1] Machiavelli wrote his book for a leader of the Fourteenth Century. He probably was looking upon subordinates as the B-Bs of our Pre-Industrial Revolution model in Chapter Two. However, Machiavelli is quoted frequently today. Further, many of today's leaders use Machiavellian techniques on their subordinates, whether they know it or not, and SOME are successful.

It's a bit unfair to suggest a comparison that goes way back to the Fourteenth Century. Instead, I recommend two fairly recent best sellers by Robert J. Ringer that are both provocative and hilarious—*Winning Through Intimidation* and *Looking Out for #1*. Ringer's main points are that (a) your primary interest should be your *own* self-interest and (b) everyone else is "out to get your chips".[2] Ringer acknowledges that he would rather work alone than in large groups. There's where Ringer and I differ—I want to work with others and lead them if appropriate. My philosophy is based on the premise that the effective leader MUST be prepared to subordinate his/her immediate self-interests to those of the group. While this can involve short-term sacrifices, the long-term benefits are, in my opinion, worth it.

A very recent comparison is provided by Tom Peters and Nancy Austin in their best-seller, *A Passion for Excellence*. They emphasize that the basic ingredients of managerial success are (a) pride in one's organization and (b) enthusiasm for its works.[3] Further, they identify the keys to sustained superior organizational performance as (a) taking exceptional care of customers and (b) constantly innovating.[4] Finally, they are totally committed to the philosophy of Managing By Wandering Around (MBWA)[5]. You'll note that this book is literally sprinkled with extracts from *A Passion for Excellence*. While they focus far more on the customer than I do (my philosophy is directed more toward subordinates), our attitudes toward people are almost identical.

## THE BASIS OF A LEADERSHIP PHILOSOPHY

How you deal with others is influenced profoundly by how you view the world and yourself. What, if anything, do you stand for? How are you different from the millions of people who surround you? My philosophy of leadership is derived from the following personal beliefs:

- ALL THE WAY.
- HAVE A BALL.
- VOLUNTEER FOR EVERYTHING CHALLENGING AND RE-WARDING.
- EVERYTHING GOOD TO EXCESS.

Let me explain them briefly.

ALL THE WAY is an old paratrooper term reflecting total commitment. Airborne soldiers have been taught to consider themselves special and will go ALL THE WAY to accomplish the mission. I'm committed to go ALL THE WAY, to be the best in my field, *in those selected areas I give top priority*. Right now, I'm a professor in a university. Since teaching is my primary business, my goal is to go ALL THE WAY to be the best teacher in the university. I'm good, but I'm not the best. That fact creates tensions within me—I have an unsatisfied need to get better. Unsatisfied needs are what motivation is all about (Maslow—Chapter Three).

HAVE A BALL means having fun. I'm committed to, as best I can, enjoying life and sharing that fun with those around me. In the process, I'll try to make the best of unpleasant situations. I'm genuinely concerned about many people who seem to take this deferred gratification business too far. They keep saying, "Work now; fun later on". If you wait too long to have a good time, you'll be DEAD before you HAVE A BALL. Leaders who don't know how to HAVE A BALL share their gloom with their subordinates. Wouldn't it be nice if both you and your subordinates could HAVE A BALL at work *and still provide an outstanding product*?

97

VOLUNTEER FOR EVERYTHING CHALLENGING AND RE-WARDING means what it says. I'm short. If they don't watch it, short people can live in the shadows of bigger people or even get stepped on. One way to be noticed is to step out of the pack—to volunteer. Very often, people get chances to volunteer to lead others and they pass up the opportunity. What a loss! Leading takes practice.

I don't particularly like routine, repetitive jobs. I volunteered for challenging jobs assuming that, in the process, I would be relieved of the dumb jobs. Sometimes it worked. Sometimes I wound up with a hell of a lot to do—a combination of BOTH the challenging AND the dumb jobs. That's a good way to become mediocre at everything. No objective is perfect. I still find myself volunteering today, but not so often. Maybe I've learned my lesson; maybe I'm getting old.

EVERYTHING GOOD TO EXCESS can be both misleading and dangerous because it depends on my definition of "good". I worry that, in our specialized society, people don't resist "bad" unless it's their specific job. A lot of "bad" seems to be observed and tolerated by a lot of "good" people. I think leaders have an obligation to do more than be "neutral" because they influence the behavior of others and because they have power. I realize that anything to excess is questionable, but someone has to make up for those millions who do nothing.

But how do you define "good" these days? I volunteered to fight in Vietnam twice. However, what I thought was "good" then seems to be "bad" now. I often wonder how the war would be viewed if we had won it quickly. I suppose personal objectives can be both useful and dangerous. I am reminded of the words of the Big Book, "Be cautious when inflicting your definition of 'goodness' upon your subjects." (Small Paul to the Moral Majority, 88:4.)

## A PHILOSOPHY—A BASIS FOR ACTION

I'd like to say that I applied my objectives continually and consistently throughout my life. To be honest, I didn't. I squirmed and made excuses and cut a few corners. However, they gave me a foundation for the philosophy that is described in the following chapters.

## NOTES

[1] Niccolo Machiavelli, *The Prince and the Discourses*, Introduction by Max Lerner (New York: The Modern Library, 1940).

[2] Robert J. Ringer, *Winning Through Intimidation* (New York: Fawcet Crest Books, 1974); *Looking Out for #1* (New York: Fawcet Crest Books, 1977).

[3] Tom Peters and Nancy Austin, *A Passion for Excellence* (New York: Random House, 1985), p. xix.

[4] *Ibid.*, p. 4.

[5] *Ibid.*, p. 6.

# CHAPTER FIVE

# THE LEADER DECLARES AND SHARES

FIRST COMMANDMENT: Thou shalt develop a personal philosophy of leadership, share part of it with thy subordinates and live by it, recognizing that thou canst fool none of the people none of the time.

"The development of a sound philosophy of management for oneself is . . . the most practical self-development project that an executive can undertake."

Ralph C. Davis[1]

The quote, above, applies specifically to people in high places. The purpose of this chapter is to convince you that every leader, regardless of status and level in the organization, should develop a basic philosophy for dealing with people. Further, part of that philosophy should be shared with subordinates. When this is done properly, the organization, the subordinates AND the leader all benefit.

**COMMENT:**
Take the case of the recent arrival of Horatio Hornay, the new President of Insufferable Insurance. The entire company is buzzing with interest since Horatio's predecessor was summarily retired ten years early because of some disastrous decisions and questionable practices.

Mr. Hornay is welcomed at a large reception in his honor. Pleasantries are exchanged. Horatio makes a few vague comments that seem a bit "hollow" since they include praise for the previous president. However, most Insufferable employees depart the reception pleased and comforted. The consensus is, "He's a fine looking fellow with an engaging smile—however, did you notice the glassy look in his right eye?" The work force returns to its duties, which include PLEASING THE BOSS.

Weeks later, Insufferable employees still know very little about Mr. Hornay. His pleasant disposition and engaging smile have been shared with all, but his views on how he wants things done remain a mystery. People go about their business as usual, generally GUESSING AT WHAT THE BOSS WANTS. Many who are ambitious "play it safe" and do a lot of silly things to gain favor.

After several months of uncertain tranquility and marginal productivity, things begin to "hit the fan". The pleasant fellow with the engaging smile stops smiling. His glassy right eye is dubbed the "stink eye". Visits to the President's office become terror-filled experiences. Horror stories of beratings of capable, well-meaning employees race through the grapevine. What follows is a prolonged period of indecision, confusion, wasted time and effort, and sagging morale as the company adapts to the leadership style of its new President—months after his assumption of office and his impact on the organization.

## THE NEED FOR A PHILOSOPHY

Events similar to those in the case, above, are not uncommom. They reflect a critical act of omission by the leader—A FAILURE TO TELL PEOPLE WHO HE/SHE IS AND WHAT HE/SHE WANTS. Each leader is a COMPLEX PERSON—distinct and different from every other person. Unless the leader has no power at all, his/her uniqueness will influence the working environment and, thus, the subordinates' lives. Like it or not, one of their jobs is to please the leader. When they have no idea of his/her preferences, priorities, methods or goals, they work in the dark. Working in the dark is both unproductive and dangerous. To quote from the Big Book, "Semi-darkness is fine for intimate moments and dirty restaurants where the food is bad, but, in the workplace, let there be light." (Small Paul to the Proctologists, 15:77.)

## THE NEED TO ARTICULATE A PHILOSOPHY

Developing a personal philosophy of leadership is only a part of the job. If the information is to be of any value to those who serve you, they have to know what it is—at least part of it. There are a variety of ways you can transmit it—orally or in writing, formally or informally, to groups or through key subordinates. The big thing, however, is that the information is available when it is needed; don't wait until you're ready to retire to blurt out how you want things done.

## THE NEED TO LIVE A PHILOSOPHY

I've never been very good at deceiving people. I think those who can are in the minority. Peters and Austin agree:

People have great built-in BS meters, they've been through the mill before. If you don't believe it, if you're behaving in an even slightly manipulative fashion, they'll see through you in a flash.[2]

If your philosophy is to have any significance, it must be the basis for your working way of life. If you find it necessary to change your philosophy for various reasons, let people know and make the change as gradual as possible so subordinates can adapt. Ideally, your philosophy is one that will attract good people and provide an environment where they can work with purpose, dignity and respect.

## COMMENT:

Some will object to my commandment, claiming that it's risky business or a waste of time. Let's examine some of the objections which come up frequently.

*Objection #1:* "I'd go to jail if people really knew my personal philosophy."

*Response:* If this is true, by all means keep it to yourself. Better yet, consider employment in organized crime.

*Objection #2:* "I'm the boss. Why should I expose my philosophical "innards" to my employees?"

*Response:* They need the information in order to serve you and the organization most effectively. Further, such action on your part can contribute to better understanding, respect, confidence, goodwill and harmony.

*Objection #3:* "I have neither the time nor the inclination to think out my philosophy. I just do what comes naturally, adapting my style to the people and the situation. Let my subordinates find out through experience. It keeps them on their toes and gives me more flexibility."

*Response:* Many leaders who share this view encounter frequent frustrations as subordinates misinterpret directions and demonstrate lack of initiative because of an unpredictable working environment. The workplace is no arena for a guessing game; let your people know where they stand.

*Objection #4:* "We've got reams of organizational goals, objectives and standard operating procedures. My philosophy would just consist of a bunch of platitudes from management textbooks that would be of little interest to anyone."

*Response:* Perhaps this is a valid observation where the leader has little power or in a static, bureaucratic organization where impersonality prevails. However, if the leader's style is likely to affect the subordinates' lives, the philosophy is important.[3]

## SOME SUGGESTIONS FOR CONSIDERATION

Examine yourself. Determine how you are unique and how this uniqueness will affect subordinates. Develop a personal philosophy of leadership, modifying it as necessary. Share a portion of that philosophy with your subordinates and live by that philosophy. Part C of this book describes how this can be done.

## NOTES

[1]Ralph C. Davis, "A Philosophy of Management", *Advanced Management*, April, 1959, p. 5.

[2]Tom Peters and Nancy Austin, *A Passion for Excellence* (New York: Random House, 1985), p. 261.

[3]Paul B. Malone III, "Baring Your Managerial Soul (Philosophically Speaking)", *Supervisory Management*, June, 1980, pp. 31-34.

# THE LEADER— RESPONSIBLE WIELDER OF POWER

SECOND COMMANDMENT: Thou shalt view thy subordinates as children of God and behave accordingly in the exercise of thy power, recognizing that power corrupts and thou art corruptible.

"We have learned how to make man worse. We have acquired knowledge how to control others—how to enslave them, destroy them, dehumanize them. We have acquired the knowledge to destroy man psychologically and morally by destroying his personality."

Peter F. Drucker[1]

**COMMENT:**
I could pontificate in this chapter, but I won't. I would sound too much like a revival preacher. If you don't believe in God, you can modify the wording of the commandment to suit your preferences.

Obviously, this commandment reveals my personal belief that most people are basically "good". I guess I'm a "softie" about living things. During the Vietnam War I couldn't really get angry with the North Vietnamese soldier who shot big holes in both my shiny helicopter and me. In fact, I admired his courage because he was in great danger too. Of course, he ruined my entire day.

Whether or not you believe in the sanctity of human beings, you must admit that modern people cost a great deal and that many of them are quite sophisticated. They are a major investment for any organization, and most of them can choose to leave you for another organization if things look particularly bleak.

## THE LEADER JUGGLES MANY BALLS

Before we go too far, let's put the leader's role in proper perspective. My commandment focuses on the leader's obligations to subordinates and tends to disregard his/her other concerns.

Most formal organizations were designed to achieve specific purposes. For most businesses, the primary purpose is profit; for government organizations, the primary purpose is some kind of service. Few, if any, were specifically designed to keep employees happy. If the organization fails to achieve its primary purpose, it will often cease to exist. Many, to include the employees, are likely to suffer.

With this in mind, the leader serves as a juggler or, as in Figure 6-1, a tightrope walker carrying the organization from the past into the future and balancing the needs of many constituencies—the owners, the customers, the employees and the general public.

## ATTITUDE TOWARD SUBORDINATES

I've been taught and I believe that God greated everyone on this Earth and that He/She inserted some good into each and every human being. Apparently, the process wasn't completely consistent; some people are "gooder" than others. Good leaders become particularly interested in studying people and adept at spotting the "goodest". Even the best leaders get stung occasionally; many people are clever at displaying their "goodness" and hiding other characteristics, at least for a while.

I believe that *every* one of your subordinates deserves your RESPECT, your HONESTY, your SINCERITY and your HUMAN COMPASSION in fair weather or foul. If you can't provide this, I believe that something should change—either you or your subordinate should leave. I don't think you can offer it to some and deny it to others. Organizations lacking respect, honesty, sincerity and human compassion are, to me, terminal cases just waiting for the cancer to run its course. Organizations *with* these foundations can develop and maintain the atmosphere of mutual confidence and trust between leaders and subordinates that contributes to overall excellence. The word gets out. People flock to join. The organization can be "choosy" and select those who appreciate such an environment.

Does this mean that the leader is a spineless jelly-fish who can't make tough decisions? Not at all. It is very possible, when appropriate, to criticize or punish OR FIRE a subordinate while maintaining respect, honesty, sincerity and compassion. Good leaders can expect AND DEMAND a quality product from subordinates. Peters and Austin note that "The superb business organizations . . . are tough as nails and uncompromising about their value systems, but at the same time they

FIGURE 6–1

THE LEADER'S BALANCING ACT

care about and respect their people."[2] "My" subordinates resent identification with mediocrity.

**COMMENT:**

Is this an easy philosophy to carry out? It all depends on you. Ralph Waldo Emerson observed, "What you are thunders so loudly, I can't hear a word you say."[3] Don't profess such a philosophy if you don't really mean it; it will become one of the company jokes. Remember that, when things get tough and emotions, particularly yours, get high, you might just forget how to spell COMPASSION. FIGHT IT! Good leaders are good fighters, particularly when fighting their own emotions.

Remember also that, as organizations become larger, there are additional levels of hierarchy, each with its own leaders. You, the top-level leader, may treat people as children of God while some of you less enlightened subordinate leaders may be running torture dens. If so, persuade them to change or fire them—with RESPECT, HONESTY, SINCERITY and COMPASSION. An IBM executive noted, "You can foul up on 'most anything and you'll get another chance. But if you screw up, even a little bit, on people management, you're gone. That's it, top performers or not."[4]

## FIGHT PERSONAL CORRUPTION

Let's face it; there are very few involuntary leaders. Certain people like power and work very hard to achieve it. They tend to get a "warm" feeling getting things done. When things go right, they get pats on the back, public recognition and nice things on payday.

Success can bring on both confidence and arrogance. Successful people "look up" (remember Maslow's hierarchy of needs); they see opportunities to achieve more and more. Their egos can swell a bit. They begin to live and act and talk and think "special". They become surrounded by hand-picked assistants who are full of flattery and lose touch with "ordinary people". In fact, they often become impatient with "ordinary people"—the same "ordinary people" who contributed to their original success. To quote once again from the Big Book, "When ye gaze upon the masses from atop your penthouse, the tennis balls way down there look like a bunch of B-Bs" (Small Paul to the Buffoons, 71:26). If they look like B-Bs, there's a temptation to treat them that way. In extreme cases, the leader might even be tempted to offer up a few B-Bs as "human sacrifices" in order to achieve some goals the leader considers important. General Melvin Zais warned his military leaders of this tendency; "I enjoin you to be ever alert to the pitfalls of too much authority. Beware that you do not fall into the category of the little man, with a little job, with a big head."[5]

FIGURE 6-2

BEWARE – POWER CORRUPTS!

"CONGRATULATIONS, MS. GOODLEY! WE WERE ALL SO HAPPY TO SEE YOU PROMOTED TO EXECUTIVE VICE PRESIDENT. I'LL BET THAT YOU HAVE SOME BIG IDEAS FOR OUR FIRM."

## SOME SUGGESTIONS FOR CONSIDERATION

• Establish an organizational philosophy based on the cornerstones of RESPECT, HONESTY, SINCERITY and HUMAN COMPASSION and insist that all in the organization live by it.

• Remember that God's children like to take pride in what they do. Aim for a quality organizational product, whatever you do. Consider Robert Townsend's advice, "If you don't do it excellently, don't do it at all."[6]

• Combat the tendency to lose contact with "ordinary people" in the organization. Set aside considerable time to wander around the organization and find out what's really going on. Never lose your ability to EMPATHIZE with people at all levels of the organization.

• Combat the tendency to overvalue your own intelligence and judgment. Insist that subordinates question your opinions and add theirs (without fear of retribution). Periodically, designate assistants to serve as challengers asking:

-"What if?"
-"Why?"
-"Why not?"

## NOTES

[1]Peter F. Drucker, *Landmarks of Tomorrow* (New York: Harper & Brothers, 1959), p. 258.

[2]Tom Peters and Nancy Austin, *A Passion for Excellence* (New York: Randon House, 1985), p. xix.

[3]James J. Cribben, *Leadership: Strategies for Organizational Effectiveness* (New York: AMACOM, 1981), p. 7.

[4]Thomas J. Peters and Robert H. Waterman, Jr., *In Search of Excellence* (New York: Harper & Row, 1982), p. 260.

[5]Peters and Austin, *Passion*, p. 292.

[6]Robert Townsend, *Further Up the Organization* (New York: Alfred A. Knopf, 1984), p. 68.

CHAPTER SEVEN

# THE LEADER SHINES AND ENRICHES

THIRD COMMANDMENT: Thou shalt not bring sadness and gloom unto the workplace. Instead, thou shalt endeavor to enrich the life of each subordinate thou toucheth.

"If you see a man without a smile, give him yours."
"Big Jim" Daniell, Chief Executive, RMI[1]

## THE LEADER AND MORALE

Life can be kind of tough without any help from bosses. The Big Book reminds us that "The leader who remains dour and sour with a glower for every hour while he wields power contributes little to the quality of life." (Small Paul to the Gloominaries, 47:11). Most people's lives are divided roughly into thirds—one third sleeping, one third working, and one third maintaining and relaxing. If a person sleeps poorly, has a lousy home life AND ALSO has a grouchy boss, he/she could be a candidate for suicide.

Wouldn't it be great if you could create an environment at work where your subordinates actually looked forward to Monday morning SO THEY COULD COME TO WORK FOR YOU? Is this practical or likely? Perhaps not, but why not make it something to strive for? I claim that, under SOME conditions with SOME subordinates and SOME bosses, work can be genuine FUN. Further, I claim that opportunities for such situations occur more frequently than most people suspect, BUT that it is up to the leader to set the stage and grasp the opportunities. Properly timed and orchestrated, such efforts contribute to improved performance and enhanced innovation WITHOUT distracting people from the mission of the organization.

Many people seem to be very uncomfortable with the terms, FUN and HUMOR. They associate the terms with kids' stuff—"get serious; it's a jungle out there". Obviously, I disagree.

Smiles require less physical effort than frowns. Laughter releases tensions. Some psychiatrists agree. In fact, they use humor in their therapy. Organizations suffer when people fail to communicate. Communication loosens up when people relax and are themselves. Everyone (to include the most exalted leader) is, to a certain degree, ridiculous. Why not admit it? Can you, the leader, tell a funny story ON YOURSELF without feeling that you've lost status? If you can't, you just might be insecure. If you can't deal with goodwill and humor, I suggest that you get a deputy who can. Check the forms used for the appraisal of employee performance in your organization. Is a sense of humor included among personal characteristics being evaluated? If not, why not?

Am I the only person with this attitude toward fun and humor? By no means. Note the comments, below, by Charles Dwyer, Director of the Management and Behavioral Science Center at the University of Pennsylvania's Wharton School:

I've seen people come from dull-as-dust assembly-line jobs who just had a wonderful day. I've seen people come in to work when they were sick and should have stayed at home. They wouldn't miss a day of work, not because the work was enjoyable or intrinsically satisfying, but because it was fun to be there.[2]

Such attitudes are not confined to academicians. David Ogilvy of Ogilvy & Mather, a highly successful advertising firm, urged his subordinates:

Try to make working at Ogilvy & Mather *fun*. When people aren't having any fun, they seldom produce good advertising. Kill grimness with laughter. Maintain an atmosphere of informality. Encourage exuberance. Get rid of sad dogs that spread gloom.[3]

**COMMENT:**
Naturally, I have selected references that concur with my philosophy. I am most comfortable among those who agree with me.

Please understand that I am NOT recommending that the workplace be turned into a playground. Properly timed humor and frivority have their place; so does serious stuff. Good judgment is essential. Jokes are a bit inappropriate when someone has passed away. Hilarity and crisis situations don't mix. However, even in a crisis, the basic optimism of the leader is critical. Subordinates watch the leader closely during such periods. If he/she begins to fall apart, they will inevitably follow. Good leaders help subordinates make the best of a bad thing. Sometimes, particularly perceptive leaders use "bad times" to turn organizations around and to achieve "good things" that otherwise would have been impossible without the identified crisis.

## THE LEADER AND COMMITMENT TO SUBORDINATES

Let us now turn to the second part of this commandment—"thou shalt endeavor to enrich the life of each subordinate thou toucheth." People who work for me are giving me part of their lives. If they serve me well, the organization will benefit. Since I am their leader, I too will benefit since my "report card" is based on the performance of my subordinates. I realize that my subordinates work primarily for money, but I feel that I owe them something more—JUST A BIT OF ME. (You'll note my arrogance here; I consider JUST A BIT OF ME worth something.)

As a leader, I have been delegated some POWER and AUTHORITY. Part of that will be used to get the job done. There is usually some left over which is available to develop subordinates. I feel that it is my obligation to take the time and trouble to help each of my direct subordinates grow and become more of a person. If they are not interested, I back off immediately. I realize that some people want very much to be left alone. They give me more time for those who will accept my help.

My motives are only partially altruistic. For most subordinates, my investment is well worth the cost in the form of loyalty and enhanced personal performance. Further, I am often grooming someone to fill my shoes when I move on (presumably, to bigger and better things). Of course, I just might groom a subordinate to pass me by. If this happens often, perhaps it's time for me to leave anyway.

This personal commitment has cost me a great deal of time in the past. If you're going to help people grow, you have to take the time to get to know them. You run the risk of overstimulating their expectations or going beyond your qualifications regarding good advice. Despite these limitations, I believe that this approach is far better than the "use them and leave them sweaty" philosophy of dealing with people. According to the recent best-seller, *In Search of Excellence*, particularly excellent companies in this country incorporate into their corporate cultures messages that say, " 'respect the individual', 'make people winners', 'let them stand out', 'treat people as adults' ".[4]

## SOME SUGGESTIONS FOR CONSIDERATION

● Develop an awareness of how you appear to other people; work on an image of good will, confidence and optimism (don't go so far as arrogance; that brings lumps).

● Find a place to hide when you're really "down". Find a confidant who can help you over the rough spots.

- Encourage and stimulate a working environment where good-natured humor (watch out for the kind that hurts people) is accepted and used frequently. Set aside time for humor and frivolity. If your organization is small, consider designating a "greeter" (a well-liked and charming person who encounters employees as they arrive at and depart from work).

- Develop in the organization a general "up-beat" attitude where most people feel like "winners".

- Seek occasional opportunities to introduce variety or novelty into workplace activities so long as they are not considered "childish" by subordinates. Ask for ideas from others regarding how this might work. Give your people pleasant milestones to look forward to.

- Know all of your *immediate* subordinates by their first names. Know something about their personal lives and their aspirations unless they prefer otherwise. Set aside time to talk with them informally about themselves. Develop some system which recognizes them AS INDIVIDUALS (consider recognition or even a day off on their birthdays).

- Commit yourself to the growth and development of those subordinates you feel deserve it. Be prepared to justify your decision concerning who gets such attention and who doesn't.

- Be prepared to make sacrifices in the best interests of your subordinates.

## COMMENT:
Robert Townsend's words seem quite appropriate at this point: "True leadership must be for the benefit of the followers, not the enrichment of the leaders. In combat, officers eat last."[5]

## NOTES

[1]Thomas J. Peters and Robert H. Waterman, Jr., *In Search of Excellence* (New York: Harper & Row, Publishers, 1982), p. 243.

[2]"Why Many Good Workers Turn into Bad Bosses", *U.S. News & World Report*, January 23, 1984, pp. 71, 72.

[3]Peters and Waterman, *Excellence*, p. 291.

[4]*Ibid.*, p. 277.

[5]Robert Townsend, *Further Up the Organization* (New York: Alfred A. Knopf, 1984), p. 122.

CHAPTER EIGHT

# THE LEADER GUIDES AND DELEGATES

FOURTH COMMANDMENT: Thy mind shalt dwell in the future whenever possible. Thou shalt not make a decision a subordinate could make just as well.

"There is increasing evidence that one of the objectives most wanted by working men and women at all levels in our times is freedom from supervision."

David S. Brown[1]

**COMMENT:**
To many, this commandment constitutes the proverbial "unnatural act". "Hell, I've worked my tail off for years so I could make the decisions. Now that I have practice, I can make better decisions than those below me. Are you suggesting that I give all of this up?"

Some of it. You've been complaining for years that you're too busy to plan ahead or to get to know your subordinates. Relax just a bit and let your troops use their brains, at least for the day-to-day decisions.

## THE LEADER'S ROLE AS A PLANNER AND NAVIGATOR

Planning, making decisions NOW concerning the future, is considered THE PRIMARY function of management. Despite its primacy, very often it's done poorly. Often leaders are "too busy"; they spend all of their time "putting out today's fires". Under such conditions, the future creeps up on them, they are unprepared, and everyone suffers. Planning for the future is tougher than making short-range decisions. It is impossible to predict the future accurately. Leaders who are noted for being "right" don't like to be discovered "wrong" when something unanticipated happens. Sometimes leaders become so frustrated that they delegate planning to staff specialists or even outside consultants. To my mind, that's wrong; that's what leaders are supposed to do. They should be personally involved *while including others in the organization in the process*. They should "unload" the relatively trivial, day-to-day stuff.

"The future", as such, means different things to different people. Top-level executives may be dealing with plans concerning events five to ten years hence. A foreman's "future" perspective may be limited to several months. The boss must plan first since his/her plans influence "the future" for subordinate leaders and planners. Despite differences in timing and scale, the principle should be the same—let subordinates have as much decision making power as they can tolerate so that the leader can lead the planning process.

## SOME ADVANTAGES TO DELEGATION

We have commented that delegating decision making authority to subordinates frees the leader to do "bigger things". There are many other advantages, most of which are quite obvious. The following statements are generally true.

• People who don't have to "check their brains" as they enter the workplace take greater interest in their work, grow as they get practice making decisions, develop creativity and, with a little bit of luck, resemble "motivated workers" (committed to improving performance).

• People who are allowed to use their brains are flattered, their egos are boosted, they feel good about themselves, their morale is high.

• People who use their brains at work frequently feel good about their organization and tell others. The word gets out: "the organization is a good place to work". The organization can be "choosy" concerning whom it hires. It can hire others who use their brains effectively.

• The boss has an opportunity to interact with many subordinates during the planning process (note that the leader should *not* allow the planning activity to isolate him/her from others in the organization).

## SOME CAUTIONS ABOUT DELEGATION

Obviously, giving away power involves risks because the leader CANNOT DELEGATE RESPONSIBILITY and ACCOUNTABILITY. Listed below are some vital considerations:

• If you, the leader, are basically insecure, delegation just might do you in. Your boss might discover the talent of your subordinates and replace you with someone who is better qualified to make decisions.

• If people are used to having others make decisions for them, don't expect them to respond to opportunities to make decisions immediately. Introduce the concept slowly and cautiously so they can adapt.

● Some people either don't want or can't handle decision making power. Find out who they are and let them follow others. However, don't make premature judgments; many people are better than you think when given a chance and a little practice.

● If subordinates are delegated decision making power and then later you take it away from them, be prepared for some resentment.

● Keep the critical decisions where the consequences of mistakes are catastrophic to yourself. Obviously, the aircraft commander of a Strategic Air Command B-52 bomber should not be allowed to decide to start World War III.

● Don't delegate all of the unpopular decisions to subordinates. That's gutless; make those yourself and take full responsibility. Of course, get help from subordinates in making those decisions; often they can come up with ways to reduce the "sting".

● Watch out for *SUB-OPTIMIZATION*—decision making based on the WRONG OBJECTIVES. Delegate decisions down the organization as far as you can to the person who has *all three* of the following:

-Basic judgment and intelligence and a willingness to make a decision.

-Complete information regarding the decision.

-*Objectivity* concerning the goals of the *entire organization*.

## COMMENT:

Take the case of Sugar Sweetchops, President of Sugar's Social Services, Inc. (massage parlors, traveling entertainment, specialized catering, etc.)— "Let Sugar's Sweeten and Stimulate Your Life". After several years of booming business, Sugar was forced to declare bankruptcy.

At the bankruptcy proceedings, Sugar wailed, "I got suckered in by a crummy management course I took. Everyone's teaching "participative management; delegate decisions to subordinates". Well, I believed them. I delegated decisions on how much to pay our people to my Vice President for Personnel, Chastity Cherwini. That misguided wretch went and paid our people so much money—way more than the going rate—that we went broke."

Sugar's problem was sub-optimization. As Vice President for Personnel, Chastity assumed her goals were hiring and keeping people. High pay rates made sense. However, the goals of the organization were *profit*. Chastity wasn't "objective"—she was making decisions based on the *wrong* goals. Sugar goofed, but now she has learned her lesson and is running a string of "way out" nursing homes.

## SOME SUGGESTIONS FOR CONSIDERATION

● Attempt to attract and retain "good" people who can and will use their brains. If this isn't possible, at least identify AND REWARD those who can with freedom and decision making authority. Recognize good decisions by subordinates. Recognize also bad decisions and attempt to use them as vehicles for learning.

• Attempt to make your mind "future oriented". Become personally involved in the planning process involving as many of your subordinates as practicable. Include in the planning process plans for the training and development of subordinates.

• Provide your subordinates the results of your planning efforts—THE MISSION OF THE ORGANIZATION, THE GOALS, THE OBJECTIVES and THE STRATEGIES. Recognize the NO PLAN GOES ACCORDING TO PLAN and update plans when things change.

• Delegate all but the critical decisions down the organization as far as possible to people who have the basic necessary ingredients—(a) ABILITY AND WILLINGNESS TO MAKE DECISIONS, (b) NECESSARY INFORMATION and (c) OBJECTIVITY.

• Consider, at least for your managers and professionals, techniques such as Management by Objectives (where your subordinates identify THEIR OWN objectives and, with your approval, work to achieve them) and Management by Exception (where subordinates are essentially "left alone" so long as their performance remains within preestablished limits).

• When time permits, try to involve as many people as possible in decisions that will affect their working lives. Include the "ordinary" working people in the process. People are discovering that "ordinary folks" have great ideas when bosses bother to ask. Consider the use of Quality Circles, a formalized technique of group problem-solving that involves low-level employees.

• Organize committees that include representatives of all levels of the organization and all specialized activities, and give them both planning and decision making functions.

• If subordinates turn to you for too many decisions, insist that they make the decisions themselves.[2]

• Since you are delegating a great deal of your power to others, make sure that you have a system where you are receiving factual and timely information about the organization. However, resist the temptation to use this information system to intervene personally when minor (tolerable) deviations from the plan become apparent.

## NOTES

[1]David S. Brown, *Managing the Large Organization* (Mt. Airy, MD: Lomond Books, 1982), p. 23.

[2]Kenneth Blanchard and Spencer Johnson, *The One Minute Manager* (New York: William Morrow and Company, Inc., 1982).

# THE LEADER PROVIDES THE "WHY"

FIFTH COMMANDMENT: Thou shalt not direct thy subordinates without explaining WHY.

"Remember, gentlemen, an order that can be misunderstood will be misunderstood."

Helmuth von Moltke

## LEADERS AND THE DECISION MAKING PROCESS

This commandment focuses on the process of translating decisions into action. What appears to be a very very simple procedure often isn't. Murphy's Law ("If anything can go wrong, it will at the worst possible time") applies far too often. Who is responsible when this happens? The leader. Why do such things happen so frequently? Often people don't know WHY they are doing things.

Most decisions involve three basic dimensions:

● WHAT the decision is. This includes WHO is affected, WHEN the decision is to be implemented and the WHERE of the decision, if appropriate.

● HOW to carry out the decision.

● WHY the decision was made.

Many leaders confine their attention to the WHAT and HOW of decisions. Often they go into nauseating detail telling qualified subordinates HOW to do their jobs. More important, many keep the WHY of the decision to themselves under the assumption that "it's none of their (the subordinates') business; they're just supposed to do what they're told." I think that this approach is dead wrong and that those who apply it pay a high price.

Mature people need to have some meaning in their lives. This need particularly applies to their work. The German philosopher, Nietzsche, observed that "He who has a why to live for can bear almost any *how*".[1] The book, *In Search of Excellence*, included an observation that "The excellent companies seem to understand that *every* man seeks meaning."[2] When this meaning is missing, people either "shut down" completely or they behave like robots. Robots can be very stupid. Further, they can become dangerous when things don't go according to plan.

## HOW TO TRANSMIT THE "WHY" TO SUBORDINATES

The most effective way to let subordinates know what's going on and why is to allow them to participate in the decision making process. This relates to the Participative Leadership style we discussed in Chapters One and Four. Many feel that this is the "only way to go". John Naisbitt observed that "People whose lives are affected by a decision must be part of the process of arriving at that decision."[3] Subordinates who have a hand in making a decision are likely to be (a) well informed and (b) readily committed to a decision they helped "author". Further, the leader has given their egos a boost and has given them practice using their minds. Japanese styles of leadership emphasize the involvement of many people, to include subordinates from many levels of the organization, in the decision making process.[4]

Despite the obvious advantages of participative decision making, such an approach is often impractical. Frequently, the decision must be made quickly; participation takes time. In certain situations, it is impossible to assemble subordinates and to allow them to participate. Sometimes, the information that must be applied to the decision just can't be shared. Finally, some bosses just don't consider it "right" to share power with "lowly" subordinates. In such cases, the WHY of decisions must accompany the decisions themselves.

## WHY THE "WHY" IS NECESSARY

An amazing number of orders issued by established leaders are ignored or completely misinterpreted by subordinates. Let's examine some of the reasons WHY this is true.

● Some times the decision appears to force subordinates to go beyond the provisions of "the contract" or what Barnard called the "zone of indifference" (Chapter One). If subordinates don't feel that the decision is "right" (according to their perceptions of what they owe the organization), they are likely to refuse to comply.

● Often the leader assumes ("Assumption is the mother of foul-ups" - Tylk's Law) that subordinates have access to information that makes the decision "logical". This is often not the case. Whereas the leader may

FIGURE 9–1

## WHY THE "WHY" IS IMPORTANT

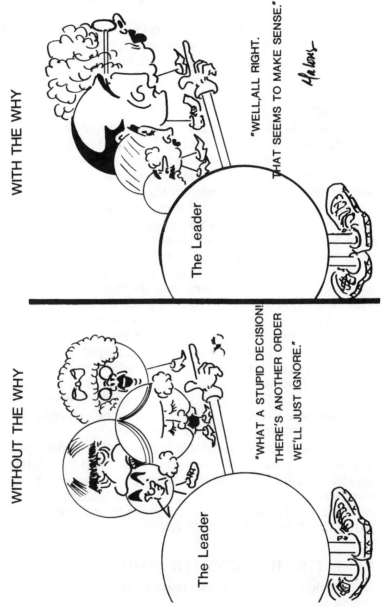

be dealing with current facts, subordinates may view the world based on outdated or incorrect rumors provided by the grapevine. What appears to be "logical" to the leader may appear stupid or threatening to subordinates.

• In many cases, subordinates receive so many orders that they must make personal decisions as to which to comply with. When this happens, they're likely to select those that they prefer or those that are most convenient.

## COMMENT:

Take the case of Gus Groaner, plant manager at Mungus Manure, Fertilizer and Associated Products, Inc. Gus is not fond of people in general. Beyond that, however, Gus has a particular hate—smoking, smokers and any kind of tobacco products. Gus groans audibly in restaurants when people light up; his behavior when passing through smoking sections of commercial aircraft has been classified as "malevolent". In fact, Gus claims that the root cause of World War II was tobacco. He notes that Roosevelt, Churchill and Stalin all smoked something, and he is sure that Hitler was a secret tobacco chewer.

Three break locations, A, B and C, are available to employees at Mungus. Over time, the smokers have gravitated to break area B. In fact, they have brought in old furniture to make the area more comfortable. Gus has refused to enter the area because of the smoking and has been critical of the smells and cigarette butts in the vicinity.

Unknown to the employees, a large consignment of a new, highly combustible liquid used in the manufacture of fertilizers has been delivered to Mungus. Since storage space is limited, Gus elects to store the product in the room next to break area B. Because of the obvious fire hazard, Gus distributes a notice that smoking will not be permitted in break area B and posts "No Smoking" signs in the area.

The smokers are sure that this is just another subterfuge by Gus to give smokers a hard time. They don't know about the fire hazard since Gus hasn't bothered to tell them. Naturally, they disregard the order since their "inalienable rights" to smoke have been violated. After a while, the whole plant, to include Gus and all of the employees, blows up BECAUSE GUS DIDN'T BOTHER TO EXPLAIN WHY.

## BENEFITS THAT GO WITH "WHY"

Listed below are what I think the leader gains when he/she goes to the trouble to explain WHY.

• Acceptance of the decision by subordinates is likely to be quicker and more complete.

- If problems arise, dialog between the leader and the subordinates is likely to be more productive.
- If deviations from the plan occur, subordinates can make accurate adjustments without necessarily consulting with the leader.
- Sharing information with subordinates satisfies their ego needs and stimulates their interest in the work.

## SOME SUGGESTIONS FOR CONSIDERATION

- Keep channels of communication open. Make sure that the mission, goals and objectives of the organization are understood by subordinates. Keep them informed of changes that are likely to influence decisions affecting them.
- Empathize with subordinates. Be sure that you view "the contract" the same way they do.
- Whenever possible and practicable, include subordinates in the decision making process.
- Go to *extraordinary* efforts to explain the WHY of decisions that
  -Involve major change from past procedures.
  -Involve "bad news" for subordinates.
- Follow up with subordinates after decisions have been made. Ask questions to determine if subordinates understand WHY they are doing things. Make adjustments, if necessary, explaining WHY.

**COMMENT:**
I found the first three paragraphs of the military Five Paragraph Field Order format to be an ideal sequence for issuing a decision to subordinates.

- SITUATION - Explain the external factors that have contributed directly to the decision, focusing particularly on changes from the past.
- MISSION - Explain what your organization is attempting to do—WHY this decision is necessary.
- EXECUTION - Explain WHAT the decision is. Provide as much HOW as necessary (don't go overboard on HOW your people should implement the decision unless (a) they really need it or (b) absolute precision is necessary).

Of course, you conclude with "Are there any questions?" Watch their eyes; some may be "way out to lunch" but unwilling to admit it. New ideas and decisions that deviate from past practices are tough to digest. Remember that "The only circumstances that people really understand are those they have experienced."[5] If it is *essential* that subordinates understand instructions *precisely*, have them tell you what you told them and keep up the dialog *until you get precisely what you said back to you*.

# NOTES

[1]Thomas J. Peters and Robert H. Waterman, Jr., *In Search of Excellence* (New York: Harper & Row, 1982), p. 76.

[2]*Ibid.*

[3]John Naisbitt, *Megatrends* (New York: Warner Books, Inc., 1982), p. 159.

[4]William Ouchi, *Theory Z: How American Businessmen Can Meet the Japanese Challenge* (Reading, MA: Addison-Wesley Publishing Company, Inc., 1981).

[5]James J. Cribbin, *Leadership: Strategies for Organizational Effectiveness* (New York: AMACOM, 1981), p. 87.

CHAPTER TEN

# THE LEADER—A BLENDER OF PEOPLE AND PRIORITIES

SIXTH COMMANDMENT: Thou shalt tolerate and even encourage some degree of conflict, disagreement and error and combat the afflictions of doppelgangeritis, numberungus and pole vaulting over mouse droppings.

"The democratic process requires controversy; and without risk there is no progress. The idle, the contented, the slothful do not crusade for advance."

Henry M. Wriston[1]

## COMMENT:

If you sense that this is a "catch all" commandment, you are correct. At one time, I had many more commandments. Having no desire to upstage Moses, I did some combining and narrowed them down to nine. There are four basic ideas in this commandment. I consider all of them essential components of my philosophy.

## EFFICIENCY AND EFFECTIVENESS

This commandment focuses on the distinctions between the terms, EFFICIENCY and EFFECTIVENESS. Efficiency, "doing things right", is usually measured by diving output by input. Effectiveness, "doing the right things", is a little more difficult to measure. It's tough to determine how effective you have been since you'll never know what would have happened if you did something else.

In our age of specialization and specialists, there is a natural tendency to revere efficiency. The specialists go about their business "doing their thing'' very efficiently. Often they're very efficient at doing the *wrong* thing.

**COMMENT:**
Take the case of Dimitrious Drivel, PhD, an eminent scholar and professor at Ubiquitous University. Dimitrious does what all teachers do—*he teaches students what he knows.* Since he is very scholarly and wise and an experienced professor, he is quite efficient at his job. However, if the information he is transmitting is outdated or of no use to his students, he is not effective.

Basic efficiency is a necessary minimum requirement for most organizations. It is up to the leader to ensure that the concept of effectiveness is added. Sometimes, this is easier said than done.

**COMMENT:**
This brings up an issue worthy of comment. Is it the leader's job to create an organization where all members operate at maximum efficiency? DEFINITELY NOT! The leader is like a chariot driver. He/she coordinates the efforts of the horses in order to obtain the maximum TEAM results. In the process, he/she may have to hold back some of the stronger horses. It would be foolish for an organization to demonstrate its efficiency by producing far more of a product than it can ever sell.

## DEALING WITH CONFLICT AND ERROR

Many leaders go to extraordinary efforts to keep organizational conflict and error to a minimum. The principles of bureaucracy reinforce this approach. Conflict is considered "bad"; it upsets people and distracts them from getting the job done. Error is considered even "badder"; it violates the whole idea of efficient operations.

Recent research has revealed that conflict is a natural phenomenon among human beings and that a controlled degree of conflict is "good" for an organization. Conflict stimulates difference of opinion and, thus, creative and innovative thought. When conflict is tolerated, people communicate openly and freely and "ventilate" thoughts that would otherwise remain bottled up within them. Organizations that suppress conflict totally usually have to wait until people literally "blow up" before they discover what's wrong. Robert Townsend observed, "If you're the boss and your people fight you openly when they think you're wrong— that's healthy."[2]

I'm sure you have heard of such things as Zero Defects Programs. The term makes me uncomfortable because it is misleading; people are human beings and human beings make mistakes—there just isn't any error-free environment except perhaps Heaven. People can learn a great deal from mistakes—more than they do without them. To quote from the Big Book, "Watch out for the bloke who has never made a mistake. He's probably arrogant as hell, and his first one is likely to be a lulu." (Small Paul to the Perfectionists, 57:19.)

No major achievement was ever made without some error. The willingness to accept some error is an essential precondition to any progress. Heinz's highly successful frozen foods subsidiary, Ore-Ida, has developed a concept termed "perfect failure". Recognizing that all progress involves risks, errors or failures THAT RESULT IN SOME LEARNING are causes for celebration.[3]

Achieving a proper "balance" regarding the toleration of conflict and error is difficult. Obviously, you don't want subordinates fistfighting in the washrooms and ignoring their responsibilities. On the other hand, you'd like to know where disagreement and new ideas exist. Further, you'd like at least some of your people to learn and grow and explore and, in the process, MAKE A FEW MISTAKES. Of course, if all mistakes are followed by punishment, you won't find many "explorers" in the organization. Further, if the errors are too big or too frequent, YOU may be looking for a new job. YOUR boss will have to concur with your tolerance of subordinate mistakes.

## DOPPELGANGERITIS

Doppelgangeritis relates to a natural human tendency for people to gravitate toward others who share their own values and experiences. It's the "comfortable" thing to do. While it contributes to human "comfort", it retards the learning process that occurs when dissimilar perspectives, viewpoints and ideas are "mixed".

Most leaders have power. They often exercise that power in the process of selecting who their subordinates will be. Leaders are people too—they also seek "comfort". If they go too far and get too "comfortable", they can become surrounded by "doppelgangers"—other people who think, act, look and maybe even smell like the leader. While this may contribute to organizational harmony, the chances for new ideas—the products of differences of opinion—are reduced. Some observers attributed President Nixon's insensitivity to Watergate-related problems to the fact that he was surrounded by a personal staff of doppelgangers—people who viewed the world just as he did.

If innovation and creativity are essential to the organization, leaders must take steps to ensure that the criteria used to select and promote people relate to the work itself and, equally important, are not so restrictive that only doppelgangers are eligible. This means that leaders must develop some flexibility and be alert to the natural talents that exist in some people who may be a bit "different". To quote again from the Big Book, "Some creative people may not fit your image of the 'ideal'. The absent-minded man who pulls out his tie and wets his pants just may be a creative genius." (Small Paul to the Innovationists, 47:32).

## NUMBERUNGUS

Don't bother to look for this word in the dictionary; I made it up myself. It refers to a product of Scientific Management—a blind reverence for and dedication to numbers and quantitative analysis in the measurement of organizational results. It assumes that management is a science, and that all management and leadership problems can be reduced to mathematical models. I disagree.

Numbers can be "good". They are specific and, at times, precise. They are useful for giving people direction and then measuring how well they did. They are comparatively impartial and, thus, fair. Further, they are readily digestible by computers. They make computer weenies, operations researchers and number crunchers very happy. In fact, these people lose their jobs when bosses don't use numbers.

Numbers can be "bad". They can be misleading. They can make imprecise things appear to be precise. They can be used to "simplify" unquantifiable subjects. They can make people lazy; with numbers available, one doesn't have to ask the question, "why". Since the "best" (most accurate) numbers are relatively short-term, they tend to encourage people to focus on short-term results. Problems in the U.S. auto industry have been attributed to extraordinary focus on short-term profits at the expense of long-term prospects. I agree with Norman Lear who wrote that

> America is suffering from an unhealthy emphasis on success as measured by The Numbers. The tendency to boil the world down into analytic abstractions distorts and oversimplifies the richness of life. It insists upon evaluating the world through ratings and lists, matrices and polls, the bottom line, winners and losers.[4]

**COMMENT:**
The Vietnam War provides a tragic example of numberungus in action. The number crunchers needed something to measure—something with numbers that would make the computer beep and click and spin, something adaptable to fancy briefing charts. The "traditional" measurements of war—area conquered, cities liberated, etc.—didn't fit a counterinsurgency conflict. Some very bright person came up with a solution—"Let's count dead people". Apparently, enough people cheered. Leader performance was measured by "body count". Some ambitious people did some grizzly things just to look good. Enemy body count was very high. Despite this,

FIGURE 10–1

NUMBERUNGUS

we lost the war. It appears that we were measuring the wrong thing, but the numbers *were* convenient. I suspect that, given the chance, some would be tempted to do it again.

Numbers are very useful. No doubt, they're here to stay. My point is that they must be used with great caution; they should not be used as a "crutch". The world is a complicated place. People are designing models (representations of reality) to help make complex decisions. Leaders should go to the trouble to understand what those models are all about. Otherwise, they will become the blind hostages of the number crunchers.

## POLE VAULTING OVER MOUSE DROPPINGS

The Big Book contains an admonition, "Tragic is the leader who spends his time pole vaulting over mouse droppings while the mice are eating the elephant." (Small Paul to the Mini-Minded, 33:82.) This quote refers to priorities.

People have limits concerning their spans of attention. Not everything can be Priority #1. One of the leader's primary functions is the identification of organizational priorities. Some do this very poorly. The "pole vaulters" I'm refering to don't think very hard. They identify senseless trivia as Priority #1, ignoring the "big things" that are really significant to the organization. Here, the organization becomes *ineffective*—it's doing the *wrong things*. The leader is responsible for letting this happen. As General Walter Ulmer observed, "The essence of a general's job is to assist in developing a clear sense of purpose . . . to keep the junk from getting in the way of important things."[5]

### COMMENT:

Take the case of Buford Boondoggle, Chief of the Department of Obscure Analyses of a large, Federal Government organization. Apparently, early in his career, Buford had been caught short concerning documentation of some work project. Buford vowed, "Never again!" He proceeded to document everything he did. When he took over the department, he required the same for all subordinates. A system of triple filing was instituted—just to make sure backup copies were available. All correspondence, to include informal notes within the department, were typed, copied and triple filed. In fact, these activities created such work that Buford was able to justify the hiring of several additional employees. Buford took great pride in the fact that his department was well above the Federal Government average in the use of photocopying services. As time went on, the demand for the department's services declined; they were just "too busy" with their mouse droppings to get involved in new projects. Fortunately, no one was hurt—*except the American taxpayer*.

## SOME SUGGESTIONS FOR CONSIDERATION

• Make sure you understand the distinctions between efficiency and effectiveness and give the latter top priority.

• Create an organizational environment where constructive conflict is not only tolerated, but also encouraged.

• Create an organizational environment where some (not disastrous) error is tolerated IF AND WHEN IT CAN CONTRIBUTE TO LEARNING, GROWTH AND FUTURE PROGRESS. Give subordinates tasks that are sufficiently challenging to make some error likely.

• Avoid establishing such strict criteria for the selection and promotion of people that only doppelgangers survive. Make sure your perspective of a "good" employee is both realistic and reasonably flexible.

• Use numbers to establish goals and objectives and to measure performance. Recognize that numbers can be distorted, misinterpreted and manipulated. Avoid quantifying the unquantifiable. Understand any mathematical models used in the decision making process and reexamine these often to ensure that they are relevant.

• Establish priorities within the organization, giving top priority to those factors that relate DIRECTLY to the mission of the firm. Be continually alert for the inevitable incursion of trivia ("Mickey Mouse" activities), particularly in large organizations.

## NOTES

[1]Henry M. Wriston, "Rugged Individualism", Annie Talbot Cole Lecture, p. 15.

[2]Robert Townsend, *Further Up the Organization* (New York: Alfred A. Knopf, 1984), p. 39.

[3]Thomas J. Peters ans Robert H. Waterman, Jr., *In Search of Excellence* (New York: Harper & Row, 1982), p. 69.

[4]Tom Peters and Nancy Austin, *A Passion for Excellence* (New York: Random House, 1985), p. 415.

[5]*Ibid.*, p. 285.

# CHAPTER ELEVEN

# THE LEADER—TOUGH LOVE

SEVENTH COMMANDMENT: Thy hand shalt include both a palm and knuckles. Thou shalt reward frequently and in public BUT thou shalt also possess the innards to punish in private with blinding speed and surgical skill.

"Firing people is unpleasant but it really has to be done occasionally. It's a neglected art in most organizations."

Robert Townsend[1]

**COMMENT:**
Current literature regarding management and leadership tends to focus on REWARD POWER—the use of positive reinforcement to help achieve organizational objectives. Less is said about COERCIVE POWER—the use of punishment. Regrettably, for some people in some situations, punishment is the only answer. In my mind, the leader serves as "a friend with standards". Since the standards are essential to organizational survival, those who can't comply become a menace to everyone. The leader must be ready to be "tough".

Before we go further, let me restate my biases. I associate rewards with "good" and punishment with "bad". I suspect that a few—hopefully very few—think very differently. Beware of the boss who sticks pins in dolls representing his/her subordinates.

## THE USE OF REWARD POWER

Most practitioners agree that frequent reward, usually in public, is a good tactic for a leader. With this in mind, it's worthwhile to remember that people are COMPLEX—no two people have the identical reward preferences. Some value money above all else; for others, a pat on the back goes a long way; still others would really love an office with a window; perhaps a few would like an opportunity to punch you in the nose. It would be nice if you could tailor each reward to each individual, but you have to consider consistency too.

Even an active reward system can involve some risks. A promotion ceremony is generally considered a "happy" event—*except* for those who were not promoted but believe very sincerely that they deserved it. Despite extraordinary attempts to be fair and consistent, many leaders discover that reward systems can backfire on them. As Peters and Waterman observed, ". . . people are not very rational. . . . We all think we're tops. We're exuberantly, wildly irrational about ourselves."[2]

There is an old saying (source unknown): "If you want to get something done, find a busy person." This seems to be true in many organizations. The "hard chargers" get "rewarded" for their extraordinary efforts with MORE WORK. Leaders who do this too often soon discover their "hard chargers" losing steam. There is substantial evidence that many, particularly the younger employees, value time off (with pay, of course) very highly.

As Herzberg (Chapter Three) noted, some people are really "turned on" by opportunities for job enrichment (greater responsibility, etc.). However, this isn't always the case. Many organizations automatically reward outstanding performance with promotion to supervisory positions. An unthinking use of this technique can be disastrous and can contribute to the Peter Principle (promotion of a person to his/her level of incompetence). A person may be very effective at getting the job done but very ineffective at dealing with others. Organizations should have alternatives to promotion to supervisory positions—alternatives that provide the employee adequate status and satisfaction WITHOUT requiring him/her to lead others. Variations of pay, perks, titles and responsibilities can be used to achieve this.

## COMMENT:

Take the case of Gretta Grindstone, a biochemist at Choakley Chemicals, Inc. Gretta was an extraordinarily hard worker. When she turned in a particularly challenging project a week ahead of schedule, Tim Dimm, the Vice President, felt that a reward was in order. He assembled the entire technical staff and announced that Gretta was being placed in charge of a top-priority government project. He seemed to ignore her objection, "But my vaca. . .", and babbled on with details of the project that involved a large number of chemists.

The decision amounted to a disaster. Gretta was exhausted and deeply resented having to delay her vacation. Further, it became obvious that Gretta was a "loner" and was unable to coordinate the activities of a large group. Tim Dimm didn't know his people; Gretta was forced into a position where she performed poorly; Choakley lost the government contract; Gretta found another job; Tim Dimm is now pumping gas and muttering, "Where did I go wrong?"

Freedom is considered by many to be a very satisfying incentive. The removal of restrictions affecting a person's life costs the employer virtually nothing—unless the subordinate abuses the freedom. Organizations with professionals and administrative support employees working in close proximity often run into problems. The professionals expect and receive considerable latitude concerning their working schedules—long lunch hours, time for exercise, discretion to take time off when things are slow. However, the administrative support people, lower in status in the organization, are on rigid schedules with preestablished breaks of specific duration. When this is the case, the leader must recognize the potential for dissatisfaction and take steps to explain WHY such distinctions exist.

A consideration involving rewards is worthy of note. Once rewards are offered, they are likely to be expected from that point on. Here is where the leader must be cautious. If you can't offer a particular type of reward continuously, it can be dangerous to offer it at all. Subordinates are likely to view the termination of the reward as a form of punishment; all of your good intentions can backfire when you can't "produce" in the long term.

Some bosses who get a kick out of the upbeat nature of rewarding people tend to "hog" the activity and do all of the rewarding personally. Such satisfying activities should be shared with subordinate leaders, thus providing them prestige and status.

The timing of rewards can be very important. Ideally, the reward should come *soon after the outstanding performance*. Many organizations I've observed make a common mistake. They hold off recognition of exceptional work until the person is preparing for retirement and then make a big fuss when the person is ready to leave. The process takes on the form of a meaningless ritual and comes too late to serve as a useful motivator.

Finally, if you are respected by your subordinates, your informal visits in the workplace and interest in their activities can be viewed as a reward of sorts. Such rewards go a long way and cost you nothing but your time. Can you afford it? Do you care?

## THE USE OF COERCIVE POWER

Punishment in the workplace can take many forms. These can vary in severity from a failure to reward to a scowl to a reprimand to the ultimate currently available to the leader—discharge or firing (flogging and imprisonment went out with the B-Bs). Even "employee-centered" and truly participative leaders must occasionally use such power in order to be effective.

Discipline, conformance to a code of behavior, is essential to the success of any organization. The alternative is chaos. It is the leader's responsibility to (a) identify the code and (b) see that the code is enforced. The leader can get his/her subordinates to assist in developing the code; they tend to comply more readily when the code is "theirs". The code should tell people BOTH (a) what they SHOULD do and (b) what they SHOULD NOT do. The code should be enforced. When any of its provisions are disregarded, then the entire code loses its credibility. When anyone, to include someone in high places in particular, violates the code, that person should be punished.

There are many leaders who are reluctant to get tough with subordinates who violate the code. The reasons for this vary: (a) some just don't have the heart to punish someone; (b) some fear that the process will "backfire" on them; (c) some are unwilling to endure the complex administrative procedures associated with punishment; (d) some question that punishment will achieve any benefits. These leaders often tolerate repeated violations of the code hoping that the problem will go away. Usually, it doesn't. Instead, what happens is far worse than the punishment of one individual—MASS PUNISHMENT. Based on the need to correct the behavior of one wayward employee, everyone in the organization is forced to live under restrictive rules they don't deserve. It's grossly unfair and, in time, it hurts the organization profoundly. For this reason, I feel that the leader must be prepared to punish "with blinding speed and surgical skill".

**COMMENT:**
A society that finds itself unable to punish "with blinding speed and surgical skill" often resorts to MASS PUNISHMENT of a sort. Women and elderly people in some American cities fear to leave their homes at night because of the threat of violence. They are being punished—denied freedom—because the system cannot punish those who would harm them "with blinding speed and surgical skill". The 21-year-old drinking age issue could also be related to MASS PUNISHMENT. Since SOME young people abuse drink, ALL young people are denied the opportunity.

Listed below are what I consider to be the essential elements of a good disciplinary policy:
- Make sure your people understand "the code" they are required to live by at work. If possible, let them have a hand in designing the code. Details of the code should be written in some form of employee handbook.

● Make sure your subordinate leaders understand the limits of their authority to punish.

● The "burden of proof" is on the leader. Don't punish unless you're sure of guilt.

● Every observed violation of the code deserves action even if it's only an informal comment. Delete items from the code if you're willing to tolerate them. The fewer offenses in the code the better.

● Be consistent regarding punishment, applying "progressive penalties" (increasing severity of punishment) for repeated offenses. Make sure that the punishment fits the "crime". Be prepared to temper your objective of consistency with some human judgment, recognizing that no two people are alike and no two situations are identical. Make sure that you are not allowing some to be "above" the code, particularly those in high places.

● Don't punish when your emotions are high. Angry people make a lot of mistakes. With this in mind, focus the punishment on the offense, not the offender—"I love you personally but I hate what you did".

● Give the offender a chance to explain his/her side of the story. Then, if appropriate, apply punishment quickly in private. Don't let disciplinary cases drag on and on.

● Design a system where the person being punished has the "right of appeal" to at least one "disinterested" outsider—usually higher up in the organization.

● By all means, avoid "mass punishment"—a redesign of the code to conform to the needs of the LEAST common denominator. The code should be designed for responsible, mature adults UNLESS you're dealing with children.

● Keep your system as simple and direct as possible or your people will be reluctant to use it. Remember that it is an administrative system, not a legal system. However, it should guarantee employees some rights provided by legal systems.

The real test of any disciplinary code is the acceptance by subordinates. For sure, employees will be watching closely when the leader is required to enforce the code. They will support what they consider to be "justice" even if someone has to get hurt. What can cause problems, however, is when someone has the reason to scream "foul". Then your subordinates are likely to close ranks in support of the person who has been "wronged". It's the American way.

**COMMENT:**
Take the case of Desi DeSade, supervisor of the day shift of some 30 employees at an assembly plant. Desi is, by nature, a hot-tempered boss. However, today, he is really "up tight". It seems that his wife, Dudu, made

some unflattering reference to his manhood yesterday when he observed her in the grocery store squeezing the grocer rather than the toilet paper.

Who arrives at work 45 minutes late but Vicki Victimnitzi, a tiny, nervous woman who is obviously in poor health. This is her third late arrival this month. Desi jumps all over her "like white on rice" gesturing and screaming with great vengeance. The noise is so apparent that other employees shut down the machinery and observe the scene in stony silence. Desi sends Vicki, now sobbing uncontrollably, home and docks her a week's pay.

Obviously, Desi has done everything wrong. He didn't bother to find out that Vicki's bus broke down en route to the plant. He gave Vicki a punishment that was well beyond his authority; it was rescinded almost immediately. The unfair public humiliation scene was a "hot topic" in the plant for months; Desi's credibility as an effective leader was impaired seriously.

One final point is worthy of comment. Firing a subordinate, which could appear to be insignificant to the leader at the time, could have a long-term impact on that person's life. Society keeps records it never kept before; the stigma could follow that person for a long time as he/she seeks employment elsewhere. If you're considering such extreme action, check the following:

- Is the offense listed as a "firing offense" in the code?
- Has the person been warned at least once prior to firing?

## SOME SUGGESTIONS FOR CONSIDERATION

- Develop an awareness of the rewards that your subordinates value and the variations of preferences among your subordinates.
- Develop an organizational environment where special rewards—both to individuals and to groups—are presented for outstanding contributions to the organization. Develop systems for the presentations of such rewards that stimulate overall organizational morale and the sense that everyone is, at least potentially, a "winner".
- Develop an organizational code of conduct, including your subordinates in the process if appropriate, and enforce that code with equity and consistency. Demonstrate the moral courage to "get tough" when necessary. However, with regard to your code of conduct, be sensitive to what Peters and Austin refer to as "little marks of disrespect"—policies or situations which are viewed as degrading to subordinates.[3]
- Make sure your subordinate leaders understand their limits of authority to reward and punish. Back them up when they're "right". Be prepared to serve as a mediator and a judge in questionable cases.

LOVE 'EM AND LEAD 'EM

• Provide for a probationary period for new employees wherein employment can be terminated quickly, simply and WITHOUT PRE- JUDICE in the event the "chemistry" between the employee and the organization doesn't work out.

## NOTES

[1]Robert Townsend, *Further Up the Organization* (New York: Alfred A. Knopf, 1984), p. 76.

[2]Thomas J. Peters and Robert H. Waterman, Jr., *In Search of Excellence* (New York: Harper & Row, 1982), pp. 55, 57.

[3]Tom Peters and Nancy Austin, *A Passion for Excellence* (New York: Random House, 1985), p. 231.

# CHAPTER TWELVE

# THE LEADER—A FRIEND IN NEED BUT NOT TOO CLOSE

EIGHTH COMMANDMENT: While thou shalt maintain some "psychological distance" from thy subordinates, thou shalt make thyself available to those in trouble, offering thy hand, thy ear, thy heart and thy handkerchief but never thy money. In the process, thou shalt resist the temptation to play God or psychiatrist unless thou art properly anointed or qualified.

"To do our fellow men the most good in our power, we must lead where we can, follow where we cannot and still go with them, watching the favorable moment for helping them to another step."

Thomas Jefferson[1]

## "THE DISTANCE"

Obviously, my philosophy of leadership suggests an attitude of caring, concern and commitment to subordinates. Such a philosophy is likely to get the leader "close" to his/her people. The question becomes, "How close?"

I contend that the leader must, in order to remain effective, maintain some "psychological distance" from those who must respond to his/her directions and, on occasions, receive his/her criticism. The leader who is "just one of the fellows" one day is likely to have problems making an unpopular decision the next. Ideally, the leader should be just a little "special". C.P. Snow observed:

Some men cannot be leaders for the simple fact that they do not care to be anything more than natural and neutral. To be an influence in any society, in fact, one can be a little different, but only a little; a little above one's neighbors, but not too much.[2]

Perhaps Snow's comment, above, overstates the point I'm trying to make, but it's worthy of consideration. The leader who becomes too "close" is likely to be accused of discrimination.

**COMMENT:**
Take the case of Vernon Vermin, the supervisor of twenty people, ten men and ten women. Over a period of time, Vernon propositions four of the women. Two tell him to get lost; the other two agree. When promotion time comes around, one of the women who slept with Vernon is selected. Who got "screwed" the most?
- The woman who said "yes" but wasn't promoted?
- The two women who rejected Vernon?
- The six women who were not favored with Vernon's attention?
- The ten men who were apparently not eligible for consideration? (we'll assume that Vernon is a fun-loving heterosexual fellow.)
- The woman who got promoted but who, regardless of qualifications, will be accused of "sleeping her way to the top"?[3]

Naturally, Vernon should be horse-whipped. He got too close; nothing he does henceforth will be considered fair or unbiased. Physical contact should be limited to a handshake or an occasional pat on the back (quite high on the back).

While the leader should be somewhat "special", he/she should have the guts to admit imperfections and even, on occasions, to point them out. Robert Townsend suggests "Admit your own mistakes openly, maybe even joyfully".[4] To me, if you can survive that test, you're well along the way to winning the respect and confidence of your subordinates. The leader should be close to subordinates—up to a point where the leader puts on the brakes and applies reserve. Where is that point? It's tough to say exactly; a lot depends on the people and the situation.

**COMMENT:**
What should you do if you are highly educated and speak the language flawlessly and you are the leader of subordinates whose language is profane and imperfect? Do you use your language distinctions to separate you from the "unwashed" or do you join them? The decision is yours. I don't think it's wise or fair to expect them to conform to your language standards. Whether or not you decide to join them, you had better be able to understand what they're talking about.

## EVERYONE HAS PROBLEMS

The Big Book says, "Show me a man who says he has no problems and I'll show you someone who doesn't pay attention." (Small Paul to the

Agonizers, 43:22.) Everyone, large and small, has problems. Your logical response might be, "Big deal. So what?" My reply would be that some of these problems affect the performance of people in the workplace. Again, you might brush me off with the comment, "What business is that of mine?" I claim that, in your role as leader, you have the obligation and the power to help relieve some of them and that you owe it to the organization and to your subordinates to try.

## ORGANIZATIONAL INITIATIVES TO RESOLVE HUMAN PROBLEMS

Nowadays, many organizations are going to extraordinary expense and effort to both address and reduce employee personal problems. They offer health maintenance plans to keep people healthy; athletic facilities and special diets to keep them trim; no-smoking plans to keep their lungs clear; legal assistance plans to resolve legal problems; child care centers to reduce anxieties associated with children; and car pool plans to simplify transportation problems, to mention but a few. Some organizations formalize this concern in what are called Employee Assistance Programs (EAP). They do all of this based on the assumption that it will be cost-effective—the returns in the form of motivated and productive employees will equal or exceed the substantial investments.

## THE LEADER'S ROLE IN RESOLVING HUMAN PROBLEMS

In my opinion, the organizational efforts mentioned above are only part of the process. Effective leaders at all levels of the organization can be instrumental at identifying employee problems, directing troubled subordinates to the sources of help and, in some cases, actually resolving the problems personally. This, too, can be very cost-effective.

One might logically respond, "Come on. Leaders are busy people. Why get them involved with individual employee problems? That business is for specialists." Listed below is my view of the logic for such an investment in time and attention.

• The leader is responsible for everything his/her people do or fail to do. If personal problems are likely to interfere with performance, the leader should be the first to know.

• Loyalty, morale and, hence, motivation are stimulated when the leader takes a personal interest in subordinate concerns.

• Personal problems interfere with a person's ability to develop. Good leaders are committed to the development of their subordinates.

• Many employee problems are created by the organization itself. The leader has power the subordinate does not. The leader may have the power to correct the problem with minimum effort.

- Leaders are often not informed of "bad news" in the organization through the normal chain of command. Listening to subordinate problems (usually associated with "bad news") often provides the leader with information he/she would never receive otherwise.
- Good leaders should become experts in human behavior. Exposure to the problems of others develops such expertise and helps the leader deal more effectively with him/herself.

## SOME PRINCIPLES OF HUMAN PROBLEM-SOLVING

Listed below are some basic considerations associated with the role of the leader as a counselor and problem-solver:

- First, the leader should be viewed as a sympathetic and empathetic friend with power and some experience at dealing with human problems.
- The leader should make it clear to subordinates that he/she has the time and interest for the discussion of personal problems.
- The leader should counsel subordinates in an environment that provides for privacy. The leader should develop the qualities of a good listener who will keep all personal discussions in the strictest confidence.
- The leader must be aware of his/her personal limitations and avoid exceeding his/her personal ability to assist. With this in mind, the leader should keep a list of sources of various types of professional assistance (psychiatric, religious, welfare, legal, financial, etc.) readily available.
- The leader should be cautious to avoid creating in the mind of the subordinate unrealistic expectations concerning the resolution of problems. However, it should be recognized that the willingness to listen is, in itself, a form of therapy in many cases. Therapists do a lot of listening as patients talk out their problems and, in some cases, discover their causes and reach solutions without further assistance.
- The leader must develop a philosophy concerning how far he/she will go to assist a troubled subordinate. Many leaders will "bend the rules" considerably to accommodate to the needs of those with problems. If you are willing to do this, you should identify WHY you did it and be prepared to respond to the question, "Is it fair to others in the organization?"

### COMMENT:

The last principle, above, suggests a basic question which tends to nag many leaders. How much time do you allocate to those who need special attention versus how much time do you spend with those who keep their problems to themselves? Well-meaning leaders who are identified as "suckers for a sad story" attract many who want to take advantage of the system. In the process, the "regular folks" who "play the game according to the rules" tend to suffer. Here is where the leader needs the judgment to separate legitimate concerns deserving special consideration from wanton opportunism.

Some of these judgments can really test your value system. What do you do if you hire a new employee and, after two days, discover that he is a chronic alcoholic? Most bosses would let him go; he is a potential liability to the organization. Take a slightly different case. Suppose you discover that a loyal and trusted employee who has served the firm for twenty years is a chronic alcoholic; what would you do? I suggest that your reaction would be different, but how and where do you draw the line?

## SOME SUGGESTIONS FOR CONSIDERATION

● Develop a personal style that stimulates the admiration and respect of your subordinates. Be approachable and congenial while avoiding any intimacy that might impair your ability to perform your duties fairly and impartially.

● Recognize that all people have personal problems and that some of these problems will influence their ability to perform in the workplace.

● Make yourself available to subordinates who seek your advice or assistance concerning significant personal problems. Remember that, as a busy boss, you are likely to appear very unavailable to deal with "incidental" concerns. Set up systems (specific times, informal visits, etc.) that bring you in contact with the "ordinary people".

● Develop an ability to serve in the capacity of a counselor with a genuine commitment to the welfare of your subordinates.

## NOTES

[1]"Leadership the Biggest Issue", *Time*, November 8, 1976, p. 2.

[2]C. P. Snow, *The Masters* (London: Knopf, 1949), p. 105.

[3]Adapted from William Raspberry, "The Charge of Harassment of Female Workers by Bosses Not Easy to Answer", *Florida Times-Union*, October 1, 1980, p. A-12.

[4]Robert Townsend, *Further Up the Organization* (New York: Alfred A. Knopf, 1984), p. 141.

CHAPTER THIRTEEN

# THE LEADER—THE ULTIMATE RESPONSIBILITY

NINTH COMMANDMENT: Thou art responsible for everything the organization does or fails to do. When things are "gangbusters", thou shalt step back and introduce thy subordinates. When everything turns brown, thou shalt step forward and take thy licks.

"There are no poor outfits—just poor leaders."
General William Creech[1]

## THE ULTIMATE RESPONSIBILITY

People who step forward and say "I'll lead" do so at their own risk. Any newsman will tell you that bad news sells better than good news. When things begin to "hit the fan", there is an almost automatic reaction among people. They ask the question, "Who is responsible?"

Some cultures, the Japanese for example, emphasize collective or *group* responsibility. In contrast, the American culture is oriented toward individual responsibility. The recognized leader, the symbol of the group or organization, is considered responsible for the organization, its people and events associated therewith. Often, this responsibility extends to areas well beyond the immediate personal control of the leader.

### COMMENT:
Recall, if you will, the prolonged crisis involving American hostages in Iran. Who would the American people have held "responsible" had those hostages been murdered? I am sure that President Carter would have been blamed by many despite the extreme uncertainties of the situation.

I am also sure that the possibility of another explosive hostage situation was on President Reagan's mind as he gave the "go ahead" to the invasion of Grenada. The point here is that the concept of ultimate responsibility can put great pressures on leaders particularly when dealing with unknowns and events beyond their control. In many cases, they must make decisions that are unpopular, at least in the short run. As T.O. Jacobs noted, they must be ready to "settle for less than universal affection. They must be willing to be unloved. No leader can be successful if not prepared to be rejected."[2]

## THE PROMINENCE OF THE LEADER

How conspicuous should the leader be in the day-to-day functions of organizations and their people? Let's look at two viewpoints. First, let's refer to the often-quoted words of Lao-Tzu writing in the sixth century before Christ:

A leader is best
When people barely know that he exists
Not so good when people obey and acclaim him,
Worst when they despise him.
Fail to honor people
They fail to honor you,
But of a good leader who talks little
When his work is done, his aim fulfilled,
They will all say, "We did this ourselves."[3]

Most would consider the words, above, somewhat idealistic and inappropriate for a fast-moving world considering the American focus on individual responsibility. Leonard Sayles expresses a very different viewpoint: "Leadership must be active, not passive; authority must be exercised to be accepted. The strong, distant, placid and silent types idealized in fiction are not the leaders of the real world."[4]

I view the "ideal" leader as a very busy and active person. If he/she is not directly involved in providing guidance to the organization, he/she is wandering around the organization finding out what's going on or he/she is identifying and developing human talent. There is no question who the boss is. There should be, however, a continual shift in focus on where the attention is.

## A SHIFTING FOCUS OF ATTENTION

Americans often (not always for sure) reward their leaders quite handsomely. Comparatively speaking, many American corporate executives receive extraordinary compensation. What's not paid directly is often provided in the form of "perks" (personal staffs, office arrangements, special privileges, etc.). The very fact that the person is dubbed with the term, "leader", is a form of reward. Of course, the leader leads a somewhat precarious existence since his/her performance is measured by that of the entire organization. However, so long as the leader "survives", the "system" is there to feed his/her ego.

When things are "good", the leader is, by definition, successful—everybody knows it. Here is where the leader can SHARE the limelight at very little personal cost. Here is where the leader can step back, place the limelight on deserving subordinates, and watch them glow and grow. That glowing and growing can contribute to future organizational success—future accolades which benefit the leader and others.

When things are "bad", the leader is, by definition, unsuccessful—everybody knows it. To me, here is where the leader meets his/her real test. Some weak, insecure leaders go to extraordinary efforts to locate a subordinate to offer as a "human sacrifice" to those demanding action. That's wrong; that's where the leader earns his/her pay and takes the lumps. Presumably, the leader's shoulders are wider than the subordinates'; he/she can absorb some lumps. If not, perhaps someone else should take over. Of course, if the leader discovers that there are problems among subordinates, appropriate action should be taken AFTER THE LEADER HAS ACCEPTED THE FULL RESPONSIBILITY FOR ORGANIZATIONAL PROBLEMS.

**COMMENT:**

The Big Book warns, "Take pity on the leader who spends all of his time blowing his own horn or allowing his subordinates to do the same. Truly great people don't need all of that jazz; they glow in the dark." (Small Paul to the Sycophants, 55:19.)

To my mind, *real* leaders can exercise humility; their natural capabilities just show through. During good times, they take genuine satisfaction in watching subordinates glow because that's part of their job. During bad times, they take their lumps with honesty and dignity because they have volunteered to absorb such burdens. They control the organizational spotlight according to a philosophy of leadership identified by Peters and Waterman: "It is being visible when things go awry, and invisible when they are working well."[5]

Take, for example, your visit with J. Wellington Barnswill II, President of Barnswill Industries. You discover that his office is a sumptuous "palace", a marked contrast from others in the building that are dingy and in need of attention. Many photographs, all including J. Wellington, adorn the walls. He is attended by a large staff that is very protective of his time. Your visit is interrupted by a series of "high priority" telephone calls. During one that you overhear, J. Wellington spends ten minutes approving the menu for an executive luncheon. J. Wellington goes to extraordinary

FIGURE 13–1

THE LEADER—A PERSON FOR ALL SEASONS

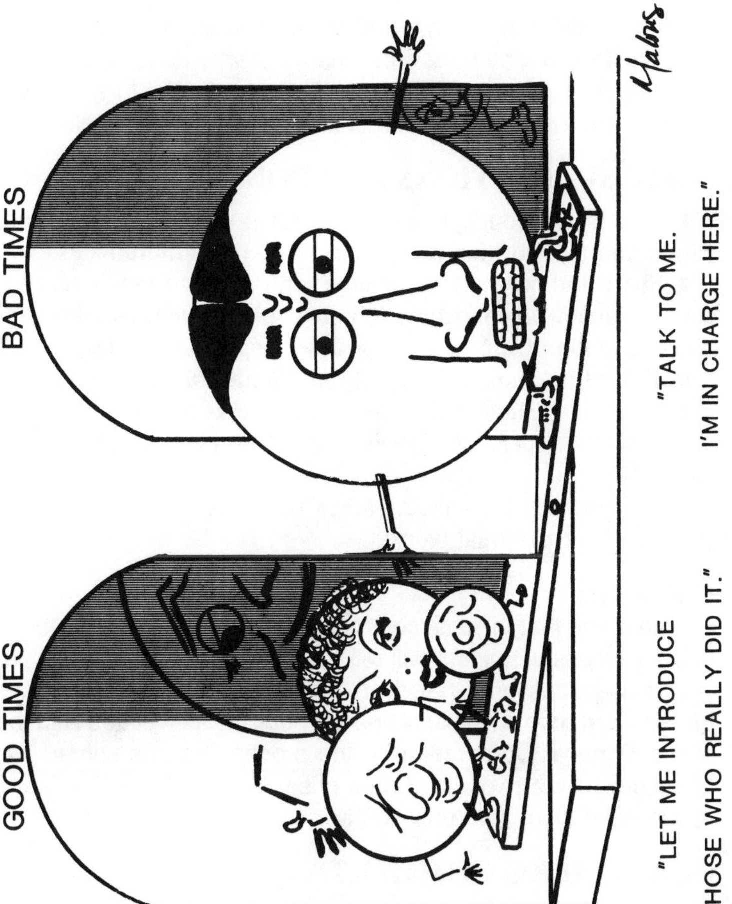

GOOD TIMES

BAD TIMES

"TALK TO ME.

I'M IN CHARGE HERE."

"LET ME INTRODUCE

THOSE WHO REALLY DID IT."

effort to let you know how important he is during his 14-hour work days and that he travels to and from work in a chauffeured limousine complete with telephone and TV. J. Wellington even gives you an idea of how much money he makes. When the subject of the recent drop in value of Barnswill Industries stock comes up, J. Wellington blames his wretched Vice President for Marketing whom he fired summarily with full media publicity. Then J. Wellington returns to his favorite subject—HIM.

J. Wellington may be a great man, but why does he have to spend so much effort trying to prove it? Is his ego so fragile? I worry when people like that are entrusted with organizations and their people.

## SOME SUGGESTIONS FOR CONSIDERATION

• Accept the concept of unconditional responsibility for your organization and the working performance of your subordinates.

• Share the rewards associated with all favorable events with those subordinates who contributed to the events. When possible, intentionally divert attention from you to the deserving subordinates.

• Take full responsibility for all unfavorable events affecting the organization. If subordinates are at fault, take appropriate action AFTER THE ULTIMATE RESPONSIBILITY HAS BEEN ACKNOWL-EDGED.

• Let your performance, rather than your words or superficialities, attest to your personal worth.

### COMMENT:
Let me admit that this last commandment is the most "fragile" of the nine. Many successful leaders will tell you that you have to "sell" yourself and your capabilities and that the selling process can't be too subtle. Lee Iacocca certainly hasn't declined the publicity associated with the recovery of the Chrysler Corporation. In the process he has served as a symbol of success for a revitalized enterprise. You might think this one over as you develop your own philosophy.

## CONCLUDING COMMENTS

There you have it, ladies and gentlemen, boys and girls; that's my philosophy. Let's hope that at least part of it appealed to you; many of the things I've said are accepted widely. Equally important, I hope that you have identified where your values and beliefs differ from mine. I've probably ignored some points that you consider particularly important. For example, I haven't said much directly about ethics and high quality work; I've approached those subjects indirectly. Further, my focus has been on the people *inside* the organization; I have said little about the essential function of any organization—satisfying the *customer*. The fact that you have other priorities and differ with me is GOOD. Your uniqueness as a COMPLEX PERSON, as a unique human being, is showing through. That uniqueness will influence YOUR philosophy of leadership. Let's now turn to Part C and work on it.

## NOTES

[1]Tom Peters and Nancy Austin, *A Passion for Excellence* (New York: Random House, 1985), p. 241.

[2]Bernard M. Bass, *Stogdill's Handbook of Leadership* (New York: The Free Press, 1981), p. 209.

[3]David S. Brown, *Managing the Large Organization* (Mt. Airy, MD: Lomond Books, 1982), p. 235.

[4]Leonard R. Sayles, *Leadership: What Effective Managers Really Do . . . and How They Do It* (New York: McGraw-Hill Book Company, 1979), p. 56.

[5]Thomas J. Peters and Robert H. Waterman, Jr., *In Search of Excellence* (New York: Harper & Row, 1982), p. 82.

# PART C

# BACK TO BERT AND BERTHA
## THEY'VE BEEN DRIBBLED THROUGH ONE MAN'S PHILOSOPHY. NOW IT'S TIME TO DEVELOP THEIR OWN.

COMMANDMENT DROPPINGS

## THEY MUST LOOK CLOSELY AT THEMSELVES.

PART C

# DEVELOPING AND ARTICULATING YOUR PHILOSOPHY OF LEADERSHIP

## OBJECTIVES OF PART C

Let's now shift gears from a PASSIVE mode of reading one person's philosophy to an ACTIVE mode of developing your own. With this in mind, Part C is organized as follows:

• Chapter Fourteen is designed to help you analyze yourself and to determine how you are unique.

• Chapter Fifteen is designed to help you develop your basic approach (philosophy) for dealing with others, particularly subordinates, based on your self-analysis in the preceding chapter.

• Chapter Sixteen contains suggestions concerning how you should articulate your philosophy to subordinates.

**COMMENT:**
Back to Bert and Bertha. They've just been dribbled through nine chapters of one man's philosophy—quite a harrowing experience. They've been given quite a bit to think about. In the process, they may have grown some. Fortunately, my philosophy is "washable"; they can retain some or take a hot soak and start from scratch. Let's join Bert and Bertha as they examine themselves in some detail and prepare to become HUGE BALLS—people movers of the Western World.

## SOME WORDS OF CAUTION

Beware! I am about to lead you into an area well beyond my qualifications. This business of self analysis is the domain of psychiatrists, psychologists and human behaviorists, and I must admit that I am none of these. What gall! I'm going to expose you to a layman's approach to self-analysis when there are real experts lurking all over the place.

My only real defense is that the price is right. Some of these professional analyses can really grab you by the wallet or pocketbook. However, many organizations are using them to help develop their people and resolve problems that degrade performance. I don't claim that my approach will achieve identical results, but I do believe that a thoughtful examination of Part C will help you identify your own approach to leading people.

CHAPTER FOURTEEN

# WHO ARE YOU? HOW ARE YOU UNIQUE?

**COMMENT:**
If you plan to "play the game" in this chapter, let me suggest that you put your mind in something like "neutral". Listed below are a series of statements. To me, they relate to some questions concerning you as a unique human being that you should address. Your responses will form the basis of your philosophy of leadership, which will be the focus of the next chapter.

## GENERAL OUTLOOK ON LIFE AND PEOPLE

Make an "educated guess" concerning each of the statements below, using the following response code:

1 - AGREE        2 - GENERALLY AGREE        3 - UNDECIDED
        4 - GENERALLY DISAGREE        5 - DISAGREE

Enter the appropriate number in the parentheses at the right. Of course, there is no "right" response; numbers will not be tallied or put to any other use.

- I am generally optimistic about the future.                    ( )
- I am confident and feel "good" about myself.                   ( )
- I enjoy dealing with people.                                   ( )
- I like most of the people I know personally.                   ( )
- I believe that most people are basically honest, decent and
  worthy of respect.                                             ( )
- I have a personal code of ethics that I follow.                ( )
- I value personal security very highly.                         ( )
- I have a strong need for personal freedom.                     ( )
- I have a strong need for personal achievement.                 ( )
- I have a strong need for power over others.                    ( )
- I have a strong need to be liked by others.                    ( )

153

- I like being responsible for things and people.                                ( )
- I like being involved with a "quality product".                               ( )
- I like things done "my way".                                                 ( )
- I enjoy rolling up my sleeves and getting involved in detailed and occasionally dirty work.                               ( )
- I enjoy situations that involve change and turbulence.                    ( )
- I enjoy situations involving disagreement and conflict.                   ( )
- I enjoy situations involving frequent crises.                             ( )
- I enjoy situations involving significant risk.                            ( )
- I appear to command the respect of others.                                ( )
- I am good at persuading others to agree with me.                          ( )
- I am an empathetic person (able to relate to the feelings of others).                                                    ( )
- I have a good sense of humor.                                             ( )
- I deal with frustration well.                                            ( )
- I am good at controlling my emotions.                                     ( )
- I am a patient person.                                                    ( )
- I am good at planning ahead.                                              ( )
- I am good at helping other people.                                        ( )
- I am good at identifying human talent.                                    ( )
- I am the best I know in my area of specialization.                        ( )
- I am able to subordinate my own personal interests to those of a group.                                                   ( )
- I am a good communicator, both orally and and in writing.                 ( )
- I can "get tough" when it's necessary.                                    ( )
- I can listen to the ideas of others and change my mind, when appropriate.                                               ( )
- I am good at separating the trivia from those things that are really important.                                          ( )
- I am an energetic person in good health.                                  ( )

## OVERALL PERSONAL ASSESSMENT

The statements, above, were designed to provide a little "structure" to your self-analysis. If they trigger in your mind others that help you know yourself better, by all means add them. The leader should be able to recognize how he/she is unique and how that uniqueness is likely to affect other people. The next exercise is going to involve less structure and call for a little creative thinking on your part—go ahead, give it a try.

1. LIST THOSE THINGS THAT RELATE TO YOU AND OTHER PEOPLE THAT YOU *DON'T* LIKE; THOSE THINGS THAT REALLY "TURN YOU OFF".

2. LIST THOSE THINGS THAT RELATE TO YOU AND OTHER PEOPLE THAT YOU *DO* LIKE; THOSE THINGS THAT REALLY "TURN YOU ON".

3. LIST WHAT YOU CONSIDER TO BE YOUR *STRENGTHS* WHEN DEALING WITH PEOPLE AND GETTING THINGS DONE THROUGH PEOPLE.

4. LIST WHAT YOU CONSIDER TO BE YOUR *WEAKNESSES* OR AREAS REQUIRING IMPROVEMENT WHEN DEALING WITH PEOPLE AND GETTING THINGS DONE THROUGH PEOPLE.

5. BASED ON A REVIEW OF YOUR RESPONSES TO ITEMS 1 THROUGH 4, ABOVE, DESCRIBE YOURSELF IN YOUR OWN WORDS FOCUSING ON HOW YOU ARE UNIQUE AND HOW YOUR UNIQUENESS MAY AFFECT OTHER PEOPLE.

**COMMENT:**

There you have it, the layman's approach to "Who am I?"

We are reminded of the case of Melanie Melange who waded through Chapter Fourteen in record time and got a "perfect score". She agreed with all of the statements; was "turned off" only by insincere men and gum disease and was "turned on" by tight jeans. She listed no weaknesses because, fortunately, she had none. However, we had to disqualify Melanie since she had previously taken a similar exercise in a popular woman's magazine; self-analysis is definitely "in" these days. Further, she was caught copying from someone else's paper. We suspect that Melanie didn't quite grasp the purpose of the activity.

As mentioned before, there are many far more complete and scientifically validated techniques for self-analysis available if you're interested. Now, while this exercise is still fresh in your mind, let's try to apply your responses to your own personal philosophy of leadership; let's proceed to Chapter Fifteen.

CHAPTER FIFTEEN

# HOW DO YOU DEAL WITH PEOPLE?

## A PERSONAL PHILOSOPHY—SOME REALITIES

If you join me in this chapter, you will emerge with some sort of framework for the development of a personal philosophy for dealing with others. There is a definite utility in doing this, but you must recognize that leaders do not ordinarily operate without constraints—they too give up freedom when they join an organization. These constraints can be particularly severe when:

• The organization is large, bureaucratic and controlled by many rules and regulations.

• The organization has been around for a long time and has a "culture" that everyone accepts.

• The organization is dominated by other strong (not necessarily effective) leaders.

**COMMENT:**
Take, for example, the case of Trudy Truheart, an outstanding young business professional who is hired for an exciting managerial job with Mother Murphy's Marital Aids, Inc. Learning that she is to assume responsibility for a high-visibility product division containing 30 employees (scientists, professionals, clerical workers and operatives), Trudy goes to the trouble to study marital aids technology and to read this book in order to develop her personal philosophy of leadership.

On her first day at Mother Murphy's, Trudy is introduced to her boss, Boswell Bomblast-Bustard, one of the firm's ten vice presidents. It seems that Mr. Bomblast-Bustard is a retiree from the U.S. Army. His richly paneled office walls are adorned with all sorts of military memorabilia to include some shrunken heads and his Good Conduct Medal. He is noted for his interminable war stories despite the fact that he has never actually heard a shot fired in anger (at least not from the enemy). Mr. Bomblast-Bustard's real military acclaim came from his development of the innovative MUCUS-SEEKING MISSILE—a missile that was supposed to home in on the nostrils of the enemy. His success was short-lived since too many of his missiles got confused and cleared the sinuses of friendly troops. He was summarily given an impromptu parade, awarded a medal and asked to leave the military service. He then teamed up with Mother Murphy for his second career.

During their conversation, Trudy enthusiastically informs her boss that she has read "the excellence series", *Further Up the Organization* and this book and that she is ready to serve as an ideal leader of people. She senses that Mr. Bomblast-Bustard might be losing interest when he begins to trim his fingernails with a bayonet. Undaunted, Trudy continues with her thoughts concerning participative styles of leadership.

Suddenly, Mr. Bomblast-Bustard stabs his bayonet into an overstuffed chair and begins to speak, "Miss, whatever your name is, I've heard just about enough of your pinko commie talk. Your philosophy of leadership is a bunch of drivel and is of no consequence here at Mother Murphy's. I'm the boss and you'll do what I tell you how I tell you. Practice your philosophy on your kids if you like, but that participation stuff will bring you nothing but grief. Now, get out of here and go to work."

Trudy's sobering experience may set her back a bit, but it should not allow her to withdraw into herself and to become some sort of automaton or an imitation of her lovable boss. If she elects to stay at Mother Murphy's (would you under such conditions?), she's going to have to deal with a challenging leadership problem.

Before we start on a leadership philosophy, let's recognize that no two leadership jobs are identical. If you agree with those in the "contingency school" of leadership (Chapter Four), this means that you should adapt your style to meet the particular job conditions in order to be most effective. With this in mind, and assuming that you can adapt to some degree, your philosophy will provide you VERY GENERAL GUIDANCE concerning how you will deal with GETTING PEOPLE TO DO THINGS—WILLINGLY. You may discover that your philosophy is completely inappropriate for a particular situation. In that case, some alternatives are available to you; you can:

- Leave your job and the organization OR
- Change your philosophy OR
- Change the organization to conform to your philosophy.

The point here is that, if you know who and what you are, you can better estimate how or whether you "fit".

**COMMENT:**
This leads to a logical question. "How much choice do I really have? Aren't I 'stuck' with MY LEADER'S style? Could I possibly be PARTICI-PATIVE if my boss is AUTHORITARIAN?" It depends on the "chemistry" between you and your boss. If he/she has confidence in you, he/she could let you do "your thing" so long as you get RESULTS. There are many examples of successful leader teams with very different styles at different levels (for example, a very EMPLOYEE-CENTERED captain of a ship with a very JOB-CENTERED executive officer).

## DEVELOPING A PERSONAL PHILOSOPHY OF LEADERSHIP

Let's, once again, do some conceptual thinking and hammer out a philosophy of sorts. Be candid; we're going to share only A PART of that philosophy; the rest we keep to ourselves. For a frame of reference when responding to questions, imagine organizations and people that you could conceivably lead WITHIN THE NEXT FIVE YEARS. Select *one or more* of the responses provided; add your own at will.

*What is your PRIMARY personal objective as leader?*
- Personal recognition and further advancement.
- Accomplishment of a particular task or tasks.
- Personal satisfaction.
- Opportunity to serve other people.
- Opportunity to learn and grow.
- Survival.
- Other (specify).

*How do you describe your PRIMARY FUNCTION as the leader?*
- Use people to get the job done.
- Coordinate human effort.
- Develop an environment conducive to human motivation.
- Serve the needs of subordinates.
- Help subordinates develop and grow.
- Establish and maintain high standards.
- Maintain contact with the external environment.
- Other (specify).

*How do you expect to spend the MOST of your time as the leader?*
- Telling people what to do and seeing that they do it.
- Discussing problems with subordinates and working out solutions.
- Planning ahead.
- Interacting with your boss and other powerful people.

- Serving as a role model for subordinates.
- Identifying and developing human talent.
- Actually doing the work itself.
- Resolving employee problems.
- "Taking the heat" from above while subordinates do the work.
- Other (specify).

*How do you view MOST subordinates?*
- Basically lazy and unmotivated.
- Basically energetic, dedicated and creative.
- Responsive to good leadership.
- Erratic and unpredictable.
- Selfish.
- Potentially deceitful and dishonest.
- Other (specify).

*What do you believe you owe the organization?*
- Total, unquestioning commitment, regardless of cost.
- A day's work for a day's pay.
- Dedication to improved performance.
- My very best.
- Just enough to get by.
- Other (specify).

*What do you believe you owe your subordinates?*
- A decent working environment.
- Adequate compensation for their efforts.
- Dedication to their development and growth.
- Genuine personal friendship.
- Commitment to the resolution of their personal problems.
- A willingness to go to bat for them when they're right.
- The minimum to get them to work.
- Other (specify).

*What do you seek MOST in your subordinates?*
- Obedience.
- Loyalty.
- Creative ideas.
- Hard work.
- Honesty, integrity.
- Genuine, personal friendship.
- Personal characteristics similar to yours.
- Other (specify).

**COMMENT:**
Let's pause a minute and recall the Blake and Mouton Managerial Grid in Chapter Four (Figure 4-4). The next three questions refer to your views concerning "appropriate" styles of leadership—the distribution of *concern for the task* and *concern for people* (subordinates).

*With reference to "the grid", what style would you PREFER FROM YOUR LEADER?* (9,1-task-oriented; 1,9-relationships-oriented; 9,9-team-oriented, etc.).

*With reference to "the grid", what style of leadership DO YOU BELIEVE YOU USE?*

*With reference to "the grid", what style of leadership would YOUR SUBORDINATES BELIEVE YOU USE?* (Some experienced leaders may have access to such information which is very valuable indeed; inexperienced leaders will not.)

**COMMENT:**
That completes the general questions. Those that follow apply to specific approaches you plan to apply, when appropriate, to fulfill your leadership responsibilities.

*How do you plan to keep your subordinates informed about the mission, goals and objectives of the organization?*

*How do you plan to keep your subordinates informed of "what's hot", the current top priority activities of the organization?*

*What standards do you plan to set for the organization? How do you plan to let your subordinates know of your expectations of them?*

*What are your policies regarding the recognition of outstanding performance? Conversely, how do you plan to deal with sub-standard performance?*

*How do you plan to provide for "downward communication"—keeping subordinates informed of events that affect their working lives?*

*How do you plan to provide for "upward communication"—keeping yourself informed of what's going on, to include the "bad news"? Do you plan to wander around a lot and discuss things informally or will you use the chain of command exclusively?*

*How and to what degree do you plan to involve subordinates in the decision making process? Do you plan to ask subordinates for their ideas? How?*

*What steps do you plan to take to maintain and enhance subordinate morale, loyalty, motivation and productivity?*

*To what degree are you committed to developing your subordinates and helping them to grow? How do you plan to do this?*

*To what degree are you available to assist subordinates in the resolution of their personal problems?*

*How do you plan to deal with change, conflict and crises that affect the organization?*

**COMMENT:**
Let's now address YOUR PERSONAL PREFERENCES, recognizing that part of your subordinates' jobs is to keep you happy. Don't be unreasonable, but, at the same time, let them know how you feel on subjects that could affect their working lives. I'll give you a few examples, but here is where your unique personality and your own ideas are important.

*What subjects relating to people and organizations do you classify as particularly "good"* (originality, high quality work, enthusiasm, pleasant relationships with customers, commitment to Equal Employment Opportunity, creative ideas, sense of humor, etc.)?

*What subjects relating to people and organizations do you classify as particularly "bad"* (carelessness, rudeness, vulgarity, tardiness, dishonesty, failure to do "homework", lack of initiative, smoking, drinking, drugs, etc.)?

*What are your preferences regarding the following:*
- The use of line and staff people?
- The flow of information within the organization?
- Formality or informality in the workplace?
- Decision making when you are not present?
- The type of people recruited by the organization?

**COMMENT:**
The final question is kind of a "catchall" summary. Forget it if it doesn't "fit" or if it just leads to useless repetition.

*What do you "stand for"? What would you like to see accomplished while you are leader of the organization? How do you summarize your philosophy?*

**COMMENT:**
There you have it, folks; an approach for developing a personal philosophy. If you've never really led anyone before or if you're heading into the "unknown", you may experience real problems providing definitive responses. Part of your philosophy should be shared; part of it doesn't interest anyone; part of it is nobody's business but yours. Let us now turn to Chapter Sixteen and discuss how we might articulate a portion of our self-analysis to our subordinates.

# HOW DO YOU EXPRESS YOUR PHILOSOPHY?

**COMMENT:**

Presumably, we have, in the preceding two chapters, gone to the trouble to respond to the "right questions" concerning our dealings with people. These should have stimulated thought toward other questions that are equally germane. Now, our task is to decide what part of "us" we will share and when and how we will share it.

## WHEN YOUR PHILOSOPHY IS NEEDED

I've made the point that your subordinates can serve you best *only* when they know who you are and what you want. This means get the word out soon. However, there are some practical considerations which must be addressed. If you know the organization and the people pretty well, you're in a position to state yourself quickly with some confidence. However, if you're entering an unknown situation or are new to the leadership business, you might want to "drag your feet" just a bit and "test the water" while you identify yourself more gradually and cautiously.

If you're dealing with a small organization, getting the word out can be relatively quick and simple. However, as you encounter larger organizations with many levels of hierarchy, more time and more planning will be required.

The organizational environment may have a profound effect on the urgency of identifying yourself. If there is a severe crisis and immediate action is mandatory, the leader's influence is required without delay. People who are insecure seek a "rock" upon which to attach their fortunes. That "rock" can be the leader who stands for *something definite*—even if that stand isn't precisely what they want.

## HOW TO TRANSMIT YOUR PHILOSOPHY

Again, there is no single answer to this issue. You should consider the following questions:

• Who needs your philosophy (immediate subordinates only, the entire organization, others outside the organization)?

• What communication opportunities are available (meetings, visits, memoranda, organizational newspaper, etc.)?

• What are *your* communication skills (good speaker, good writer, etc.)?

• Do you want to transmit your philosophy personally or to allow it to be retransmitted by subordinate leaders who are likely to distort your message?

**COMMENT:**
Whether or not you plan to talk about your philosophy, remember that leaders are often called upon to make remarks, frequently without warning. With this in mind, leaders should *always* be prepared with a brief, reasonably interesting speech appropriate for most occasions. Failure to do this could be embarrassing.

## WHAT TO INCLUDE IN YOUR PHILOSOPHY

A personal philosophy that is to have any utility should be a unique combination of candidness, idealism and reality. The leader should demonstrate that he/she has done his/her "homework", and that the philosophy reflects an understanding of the mission of the organization and "the contract" as viewed by the subordinates. While the leader shares some long-term aspirations with subordinates, he/she should not stimulate unrealistic expectations. Most important, the leader lets the subordinates know what he/she expects of them and both HOW and WHY these expectations will be achieved. In the process, the leader shares his/her idiosyncracies THAT WILL INFLUENCE INTERPER-SONAL RELATIONSHIPS IN THE WORKPLACE. Do you share the fact that you're a "nut" on punctuality? I'd say yes. Do you let them know that you find porno movies intellectually stimulating? I'd say that's none of their business.

**COMMENT:**
Let's take the case of the Bilious Bank and Trust that has been faring very poorly during a period of major transition in the financial industry. The bank is a classic case of a tradition-bound, unchanging bureaucracy. When the president of twenty years dies suddenly, the Board of Directors, alarmed about the shaky status of the bank, appoints a well-qualified

professional, Veronica Vertex, as president and gives her considerable authority.

Veronica has conducted a fairly thorough self-analysis. She knows that she's quite optimistic about most people and that she favors a participative style of leadership. In the past, she has been very successful using Management by Objectives and job enrichment techniques to stimulate employee participation. She's a casual and informal type of person who is totally committed to wide open communications and lots of innovation within an organization. Despite this, she is a stickler for high professional standards and is very critical of mediocre performance. She dislikes pomp and ceremony and is very critical of those who flaunt wealth or status in the workplace. She is extremely sensitive about questionable ethical practices, particularly padded expense accounts and expensive, "boozy" lunches. She objects violently to any form of alcohol during the work day. She is totally committed to Equal Employment Opportunity, especially opportunities for women in professional work. She prefers to make major decisions alone after considerable inputs from subordinates. She works very long hours but prefers that others do not imitate her. She is aware that she is not a particularly "warm" person and that she has a ferocious temper when provoked.

Bank officers are reserved but polite at the initial reception welcoming Ms. Vertex. When she is asked to say a few words, it becomes quite apparent that she has done her "homework". She recognizes the current condition of the bank, but establishes as an objective a recovery to number one status in the area within five years. She indicates that the bank must expand its areas of financial operations and reduce overhead costs. Further, she advises the staff that she will be visiting all of the bank branches and speaking to people informally on an unannounced schedule. She makes a major point that she favors an environment of informality, open communication and innovative ideas and that she's ready to violate some traditional approaches to leadership to achieve this. Her talk of only five minutes demonstrates her personal confidence, professional knowledge and charm and includes some well-timed humor. She is definitely in charge; her general philosophy is beginning to be revealed; the specifics will come later.

Veronica uses the next two days to get acquainted, look around and gather information. She has a long meeting with her personal staff and explains how she prefers to operate in some detail while watching for reactions and gathering impressions. At the next meeting of the top-level staff, she proceeds to go into detail concerning her personal philosophy of leadership. She assumes that some of this will be retransmitted throughout the bank but recognizes that much of it will be distorted, particularly since she represents a new order and, thus, a threat to many old-timers. She schedules visits to all major departments and branches and uses the opportunity to gather information and let people know how she operates. She spends considerable time personally developing a written statement of general goals, objectives and policies for the bank suitable both for employees and the general public. This statement is reproduced in the bank newsletter; portions are quoted in the local area newspaper.

Within two weeks, Veronica's philosophy is "out". In this case, since a major change is involved, it is imperative that people know where they stand with the new boss. They may not like what they hear, but they're not subjected to something worse—a guessing game. Those who can't "live with" the philosophy can fight back or get out. Those who can contribute are on reasonably firm ground. Now Veronica can use the feedback to "fine tune" her philosophy to fit the day-to-day realities of the situation.

Leaders have power. That power influences the lives of others. No two leaders are the same. Each leader exercises his/her power in a unique manner. That part of the leader's uniqueness that affects the workplace should be shared with subordinates. That's what a philosophy of leadership is all about.

# SAY GOODBYE TO BERT AND BERTHA.

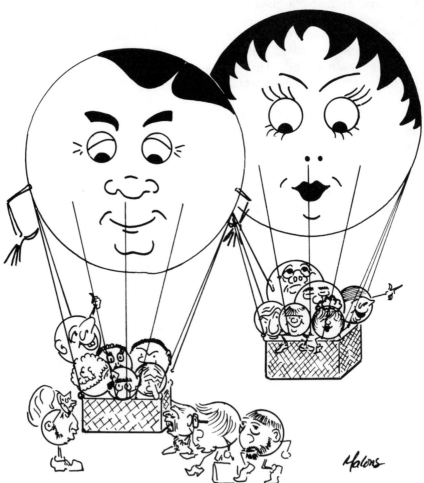

PEOPLE ARE JOINING THEM AS THEY SAIL TOWARD SUCCESS AND
ACHIEVEMENT. NOW THEY ARE HUGE BALLS.
LET'S HOPE IT'S NOT ALL HOT AIR!

# SUMMARY/CONCLUSIONS

**COMMENT:**
To quote Porky Pig at the end of a cartoon, "Well, th-th-that's all folks!" If you picked up this book and found it impossible to put down until now, YOU'RE MY KIND OF PEOPLE! (Of course, this may not say much for your taste.) I've tried to present a serious message and, at the same time, entertain you. If you feel you've been dragged through some "bathroom humor", remember it was presented in good faith; I have no desire to offend a paying customer.

## THE MESSAGE OF THE BOOK

As mentioned up front, this book has three themes:
- First, leading people nowadays is considerably more challenging and demanding than it has been in the past.
- Second, participative leadership (sharing power and decision making authority with subordinates) is no longer an option available to the leader—it is a MUST in advanced societies.
- Third, leaders must know themselves in order to be successful in influencing others. Leaders must take the time to develop their own personal philosophies of leadership AND THEN go to the trouble of sharing a portion of their philosophies with their subordinates.

The book was organized to achieve the following:
- Part A provided basic information associated with leadership and related subjects.
- Part B provided you MY personal philosophy of leadership—an example to reflect upon.
- Part C provided some suggestions concerning how YOU might develop and then articulate YOUR personal philosophy.

If you are now better aware of what leadership is and how YOU might lead people, your investment in time and money may be cost-effective. Let me now explain why I think this is important.

## "THE PROBLEM"

We live in a land of immeasurable wealth and virtually limitless opportunity. Such conditions should contribute to happy people. Unfortunately,
in many cases, we seem to be missing the boat. We've become mesmerized
by technology. Just at a time when people see an opportunity to exercise
their "humanness" and their uniqueness and their creativity, perhaps for
the first time in history, we're treating them like machines. We call them
"human resources" rather than people. We give them numbers so we
can tell them apart. As Robert Townsend notes, "Most people in big
companies today are administered, not led. They are treated as personnel,
not people."[1] Many small organizations aren't much better. Daniel
Yankelovitch comments that "The work ethic [in America] is alive and
well, urgently wishes to express itself, and is hobbled at every turn by
management." Garry Bello of Clark Equipment observes, "Management
gets exactly the work force it deserves, not one iota more and not one
iota less."[2]

## "THE PRICE"

Some would respond to the paragraph, above, with, "So what? It's the
price we must pay to enjoy the benefits of modern technology. Besides,
look at the standard of living." I claim that the "price" is mediocrity—
mediocre products and mediocre services provided by indifferent, unmotivated and often surly people. The report of the National Commission
on Excellence in Education warns, ". . . the foundations of our society
are presently being eroded by a rising tide of mediocrity that threatens
our very future as a nation and a people. . . ."[3] Robert Shnayerson
suggests that "What America needs is a fire in its belly, a brain in its
head, and the courage to halt this country's slide into national mediocrity."[4] There is no question; the human talent is out there; it's potentially
better than it has ever been before. However, it's of little value if it really
doesn't care. That's where effective leaders come in.

## "THE SOLUTION"

America is "up to here" with trained *managers*; we're short on committed
*leaders* who "give a damn" about people. We're super on *efficiency*
(doing things right); we need more focus on *effectiveness* (doing the right
things). The "right things" relate to how human beings "tick". We need
more potential leaders who know and *care* about how and WHY people
behave as they do. We need more potential leaders who are able to
subordinate their emphasis on *ME* to a genuine concern for *WE*. Is the
"solution" LOVE? Not quite. I've known some great lovers who were
lousy leaders. The combination we seek is CONCERN, VISION and

COURAGE—a genuine CONCERN for people; an ability to determine what's best IN THE LONG TERM, and the COURAGE to fight for what's right, regardless of personal interests. To quote from the Big Book *for the absolutely last time*, "If, as the leader, you can't get the job done, you can always be fired or replaced. However, if, as the leader, you despoil human lives in the process, better that you had never lived." (Small Paul to the Future Leaders of America, 01:01.)

## NOTES

[1]Robert Townsend, *Further Up the Organization* (New York: Alfred A. Knopf, 1984), p. 122.

[2]Tom Peters and Nancy Austin, *A Passion for Excellence* (New York: Random House, 1985), p. 247.

[3]Michel Crozier, "America, An Adult Nation Can't Afford Your Illusions", *The Washington Post*, July 1, 1984, p. C2.

[4]Gordon L. Lippitt, "Courage: In Common with the Giraffe", *Training and Development Journal*, January, 1983, p. 88.

# ABOUT THE AUTHOR

Paul Malone's interest in leadership began when he was a cadet at West Point. After graduation from the Military Academy, he pursued an extraordinarily active military career first as a paratrooper and Ranger, later as an Army Aviator flying a variety of both fixed- and rotary-wing aircraft. During his first tour in the Vietnam War, he received a severe gunshot wound while flying his helicopter and directing the extraction from the jungle of an ambushed infantry battalion. This wound led to a reorientation of his military career from combat unit assignments to executive-level education and development. His military service was recognized by three awards of the Legion of Merit, the Distinguished Flying Cross, and numerous other decorations to include the Purple Heart.

Paul's interest in a practical book on leadership was stimulated when he earned a Doctor of Business Administration degree and taught at the National Defense University in Washington, D.C. He has taught leadership- and management-related subjects to great numbers of students at the undergraduate, graduate and executive levels both at the National Defense University and, later after retirement in the grade of colonel, at George Washington University where he is now an Associate Professor of Business Administration.

Paul has an inborn fondness for innovation, humor and fun. His cartooning began when he was a cadet at West Point where he poked gentle fun at "the system". When he entered the teaching phase of his life, he concluded that a combination of levity and learning, properly orchestrated, *could* be a productive mix. His experimentation in this area, not without mishap, has resulted in a teaching style characterized by unlimited enthusiasm, occasional irreverence and, in general, highly satisfied customers. *Love 'Em and Lead 'Em* is an attempt to blend this philosophy plus his leadership-related experience and research into a book which is both useful and entertaining.

# ORDER FORM

**TO: SYNERGY PRESS**
**3420 HOLLY ROAD**
**ANNANDALE, VA 22003**
**TELEPHONE: (703) 573 0909**
**FAX:        (703) 698 0372**

Enclosed is a check for _____ . Please send me the following by Paul Malone:

(___) copy(ies) of *Abuse 'Em and Lose 'Em* (paperback only).
Price: $11.95 for book plus $1.60 for shipping of one book and $.40 for each additional book.

(___) copy(ies) of *Love 'Em and Lead 'Em*.
Price: $10.95 for book plus $1.50 for shipping of one book and $.30 for each additional book.

...........................................................
____ I'd like my book(s) signed by the author.

____ Please send me information concerning quantity order discounts and hard cover rates (*Love 'Em and Lead 'Em* only hard cover).

____ I can't wait 2-3 weeks for book rate. Enclosed is $3.00 per book for First Class Mail.
...........................................................
I understand that I may return the book(s) undamaged for a full refund if not satisfied.

**NAME:**_____
**ADDRESS:**_____
_____ **ZIP** _____